Hacking the Academy

DIGITAL HUMANITIES

The Digital Humanities series provides a forum for groundbreaking and benchmark work in digital humanities, lying at the intersections of computers and the disciplines of arts and humanities, library and information science, media and communications studies, and cultural studies.

Series Editors:
Julie Thompson Klein, Wayne State University
Tara McPherson, University of Southern California
Paul Conway, University of Michigan

Teaching History in the Digital Age
T. Mills Kelly

Hacking the Academy: New Approaches to Scholarship and Teaching from Digital Humanities
Daniel J. Cohen and Tom Scheinfeldt, Editors

DIGITALCULTUREBOOKS, an imprint of the University of Michigan Press, is dedicated to publishing work in new media studies and the emerging field of digital humanities.

Hacking the Academy

NEW APPROACHES TO SCHOLARSHIP AND TEACHING FROM DIGITAL HUMANITIES

Edited by

Daniel J. Cohen and Tom Scheinfeldt

The University of Michigan Press
Ann Arbor

Published in the United States of America by
The University of Michigan Press
Manufactured in the United States of America
⊗ Printed on acid-free paper

2016 2015 2014 2013 4 3 2 1

A CIP catalog record for this book is available from the British Library.

DOI: http://dx.doi.org/10.3998/dh.12172434.0001.001

Library of Congress Cataloging-in-Publication Data

Hacking the academy : new approaches to scholarship and teaching from digital humanities / edited by Daniel J. Cohen and Tom Scheinfeldt.
pages cm. — (Digital humanities)
Includes bibliographical references.
ISBN 978-0-472-07198-2 (cloth : acid-free paper) — ISBN 978-0-472-05198-4 (pbk. : acid-free paper) — ISBN 978-0-472-02947-1 (e-book)
1. Communication in learning and scholarship—Technological innovations. 2. Scholarly electronic publishing. 3. Humanities—Information technology. 4. Humanities—Digital libraries. 5. Humanities—Research. I. Cohen, Daniel J. (Daniel Jared), 1968– II. Scheinfeldt, Tom.
AZ186.H33 2013
001.2—dc23 2013001475

Contents

Hacking Institutions

Cautions

Introductions

Preface

Daniel J. Cohen and Tom Scheinfeldt

On May 21, 2010, we posted these intentionally provocative questions online:

> Can an algorithm edit a journal? Can a library exist without books? Can students build and manage their own learning management platforms? Can a conference be held without a program? Can Twitter replace a scholarly society?

We asked for contributions to a collectively produced volume that would explore how the academy might be beneficially reformed using digital media and technology. The process of creating the edited volume itself would be a commentary on the way things are normally done in scholarly communication, with submissions coming in through multiple channels, including blogs, Twitter, and email, and in multiple formats—everything from a paragraph, to a long essay, to multimedia. We also encouraged interactivity—the possibility that contributors could speak directly to each other, rather than creating the inert, isolated chapters that normally populate edited volumes. We then sent out notices via our social networks, which quickly and extensively disseminated the call for submissions. Finally, we gave contributors a mere seven days—the better to focus their attention and energy.

Between May 21 and May 28, 2010, we received a remarkable 329 submissions from 177 authors, with nearly a hundred submissions written during the weeklong event, and the other two-thirds submitted by authors from their prior writing on the subject matter. This struck us as a major success for an untested model—one that we feel could be replicated to provide state-of-the-field volumes in many disciplines, to open debate in ways that journals and books are unable to do, or to aggregate existing works from around the web on a common theme.

From this large pool of contributions we have assembled what we consider to be the best works of any size and shape (with the unfortunate exception of audio and video, which we could not put into print). Only one-sixth of the contributions made the cut; in general, we sought writing that moved beyond mere complaints about the state of the academy into more careful diagnoses and potential solutions. There are some rants, to be sure, but also many calm analyses of how academia could work differently.

Some biases undoubtedly exist in this volume. Because of whom we were able to reach during the event week, and how we reached them (mostly through blogs and Twitter), this book is largely written from the perspectives and concerns of our follow travelers in digital humanities—although this is a rather varied bunch, including scholars, educational technologists, librarians, and cultural heritage professionals. It is obviously the product of people deeply involved in the digital realm, and who look to that realm for addressing problems, rather than, say, labor unions.

We believe that the small window for submissions and the excitement about trying to reconceive how an edited volume might be put together lend this book a vibrancy and intensity (and yes, occasionally a stylistic informality) that might have been missed if we had had a standard yearlong call for contributions, followed by arm-twisting for another year or two. This volume thus represents a good snapshot of how scores of engaged academics who care deeply about higher education are trying to further its original goals of learning, scholarship, and service, albeit in novel ways that may be uncomfortable for those with a more conservative bent.

But we hope more generous readers will notice that many of this book's themes, although perhaps dressed in new technology, actually attempt to revive age-old values and methods in the academy. For instance, our authors agree on the need for open access to scholarship—not only, or primarily, because the web has enabled us to post that scholarship online, but because it has long been an ethical imperative of teachers to share their knowledge as widely as possible. New modes of engaging students in the classroom with digital media are, at heart, less about the flashiness of technology and more about the need to move past the stagnation of the lecture into deeper, more collaborative—and ultimately, more effective—pedagogy. Perhaps this is why some of the suggestions herein, such as adding "unconferences" to scholarly meetings, are beginning to find an audience.

Finally, the reader may legitimately ask: doesn't the existence of *Hacking the Academy* as a book undermine its argument? Why put this supposedly firebrand work into a traditional form? The answer is that we wanted this project to have maximum impact, and especially to reach those for whom RSS feeds and Twitter are alien creatures. Moreover, one of the main themes of this volume—and of digital technology—is that scholarly and educational content can exist in multiple forms for multiple audiences. What you have in front of you is but one form of a project called *Hacking the Academy*. The website—hackingtheacademy.org—will continue to host a much larger and more diverse version of the work, including themes and genres missing from the print edition. If this book is static, the overall project is anything but. You are encouraged to add your contributions to the ongoing conversation about how we can hack the academy together.

Why "Hacking"?

Tad Suiter

As a fan of Oulipo and Oubapo, the notion of trying to crowdsource the meat of an edited volume in a single week is particularly exciting to me. I think that imposing constraints, even arbitrary ones, can be a very effective technique that can foster creative thought, new ideas, and force one to reassess convention. Which, of course, is all in keeping with the very spirit of this book.

However, as I began to explain the project to friends outside the digital humanities, my academic friends who are not plugged into the world of computer-based methodologies in humanistic research and pedagogy, I got a lot of confused looks and cocked heads when I mentioned the title.

"What does that mean, exactly?" was a common reply.

The metaphor of hacking is central to this project. And I think it is extremely apt. But the term is a subtle one, and frequently misused in public discourse. To avoid preaching to the choir—to make this project more comprehensible and useful to readers who may be coming from a less technical background—I think it is important to talk, briefly, about what "hacking" means, and what it might mean to "hack the academy."

Popular Images of Hackers

From news accounts, film, and television, most people have a certain concept of what the term "hacker" means. And it is not a term with many positive associations. News accounts over the last quarter century have constructed a notion of hackers as a dangerous element—young men in basements, ruthlessly attempting to subvert any sense of security in the age of networked computers. Hackers endanger national security by cracking into national security networks. (Which, after all, is how the Net was born—out of DARPA's ARPANET.) Hackers are trying to steal your personal data. They want to steal your passwords, and empty your bank account. They are malevolent, egotistical, and avaricious.

Movies like *WarGames* and *Hackers* brought a more human face to hackers, portraying them as young men (they are almost always portrayed as men) who are driven by youthful exuberance, curiosity, and misled idealism who nevertheless get involved in a very dangerous game of violating security. From sources like these we get the imagery that dominates the public imagination about hackers: dark rooms, incessant typing into UNIX terminals, sometimes strange three-dimensional graphical user interfaces with which the hacker virtually flies through towers of pure information. However, all of this focuses simply on crackers—a specific subgroup of hackers who "crack" security systems. "Hacking" itself has a far more expansive, impressionistic meaning.

The Meaning of "Hack"

There are many definitions of "hack," some of them seemingly deeply contradictory. Yet there is, in the final analysis, a unity to the term. Originally, the term was used to describe computer code. There were two opposing meanings to calling a piece of code a "hack." One: it is expertly written, efficient, and does precisely what it is intended to do, with eloquence. The other was that the code was hastily written, sloppy, and essentially only just good enough. It was a workaround—the software equivalent of a hardware kludge.

As mutually exclusive as these two connotations of the term may seem, however, both the polished, impressive hack and the quick-and-dirty hack have a fundamental similarity. They are both born of a certain relationship to a certain type of knowledge.

Hackers are autodidacts. From the earliest hackers working at large research universities on the first networks to anyone who deserves the term today, a hacker is a person who looks at systemic knowledge structures and learns about them from making or doing. They teach themselves and one another because they are at the bleeding edge of knowledge about that system.

Through that type of knowledge seeking and knowledge creation, you may approach a fork in the road with a particular problem you are working on, and you have to decide to either go for an ugly hack or an eloquent hack. Either way, the product is functional, it does something, and it is innovative; also, it is a product of your relationship to that systemic knowledge structure—to the computer languages, networking protocols, etc.

The culture of the first people to use the term "hack" produced a second-order meaning, as well. A hack is a practical joke, a playful subversion or gaming of a system. The online MIT Gallery of Hacks presents a fascinating history of such hacks on MIT's campus, from Caltech's cannon mysteriously disappearing and reappearing at MIT, to a campus police car appearing on the roof of the MIT dome.[1] These "hacks" are not really so different, however, from the software hacks discussed earlier. There is a sense of play in coding, too—it is not apparent to everyone, but it is there. The fundamental action here is the same: it is the clever gaming of complex systems to produce an unprecedented result.

The Hacker Ethos

Learning about and improving highly complex systems by playful innovation is at the core of what I call the "hacker ethos." The fact that this is about a relationship to knowledge systems means that the term has, over the last thirty years or so, come to be applied to an ever-growing assortment of activities: life hacking, game modding, phone phreaking, iPhone jailbreaking, and IKEA hacking, among others.

In each of these activities, you can see the kernel of the same hacker ethos. Each of these activities is based on the use of playful creation to enrich knowledge of complex systems, whether you are making furniture from the complex system that is the IKEA catalog, or learning how to game Ma Bell for free calls to Bangalore.

This sort of playful creation should not be unfamiliar to academics. It is not dissimilar to the Situationist International's concept of *detournement*, or Dick Hebdidge's notion of subcultural style systems. It is Levi-Strauss's *bricolage* reimagined for a time when computers have replaced magic.[2]

A different approach to this hacker ethos can be found in what Eric Steven Raymond has described as "The Hacker Attitude." Raymond discusses five elements that he feels are central to this attitude, which is born of what I would describe as its general ethos:

1. The world is full of fascinating problems waiting to be solved.
2. No problem should ever have to be solved twice.
3. Boredom and drudgery are evil.

4. Freedom is good.
5. Attitude is no substitute for competence.

I would argue that a great number of academics would agree with most, if not all, of those statements, though they might not want to admit to it.

Why Hack the Academy?

Many of the entries in this project offer answers to this question. The academy is approaching a new integration with revolutionary new technology. We have quickly gone from computers in the classroom to classrooms inside computers, and to the integration of new media into the very fabric of classroom interaction. Computer-based research in the age of ubiquitous, fast, and cheap computing is changing very fundamentally our approaches to research, collegiality, and collaboration. Pure information is getting cheaper and more easily accessible, while the mental and coding chops to process the glut of information are becoming more and more valuable in the new knowledge economy.

We can see two highly complex systems—computer technology and the academy, one complex by nature, and one deeply complex by force of history—colliding and hybridizing. As this happens, we are faced with a situation where even the very clever people on the cutting edge who have working knowledge of both systems cannot fully synthesize them and predict outcomes. We do not know what this hybridization will amount to. So all we can do is steer it by getting out there and learning more by creative experimentation. You have to make the tools that steer the future of academia, or that future will be steered by whomever has the best sales pitch to the administrators. We have to create tools and efficiencies that improve the way we do things, because only by so doing can we fully understand the new world we inhabit.

In other words, we have to embrace the hacker ethos.

There is a lot to be bleak about when you look to the future of higher education. The academic job market is grim. The publishing system seems on the verge of economic collapse. Universities are quickly becoming prohibitively expensive for the vast majority of students, who are in turn forced into an exploitative system of student loans. The system, to some of us, appears to be broken.

But when a system fails, you hack around it. Some hacks may be eloquent and subtle; they may be almost poetic. Others are nasty hacks that only really serve in a single work case—but in either case, you've routed around the problem. You've fixed something. You've improved functionality. And likely, you've learned a little something yourself about the functioning of the system you're working with, and will be better prepared next time you find a bug.

The hacker ethos, in the end, might save us—or at least prolong the life of the academy as we know it.

Finally, there is that sense of play. It's something that "serious" academics do not get to explore as often as they should. Play is good for the soul—it reinvigorates, brings joy, renews commitments. It makes things fun. And it is also good for the intellect. Play leads to types of problem solving and synthesis that would otherwise be impossible. There's a reason that "clever" means both funny and smart. Reading through the submissions to this project, I think that is one theme that comes through again and again.

The academy, ultimately, can only be invigorated and improved by an infusion of the hacker ethos that goes beyond the computer science departments and infects all the disciplines. It has the potential to help fix problems in the system, deepen our understanding, and make our lives a little more fun.

Notes

1. "IHTFP Hack Gallery," Interesting Hacks to Fascinate People: The MIT Gallery of Hacks, http://hacks.mit.edu/.

2. Guy Debord and Gil Wolman, "A User's Guide to Detournement," trans. Ken Knabb, 2006, http://www.bopsecrets.org/SI/detourn.htm. Dick Hebdige, *Subculture: The Meaning of Style* (London and New York: Routledge, 2002), http://search.ebscohost.com/login.aspx?direct=true&scope=site&db=nlebk&db=nlabk&AN=67998. Claude Lévi-Strauss, *The Savage Mind* (Chicago: University of Chicago Press, 1966).

Hacking Scholarship

Getting Yourself Out of the Business in Five Easy Steps

Jason Baird Jackson

Last year, did you get paid nothing to work hard for a multinational corporation with reported revenues of over a billion dollars?

If you have (1) done peer reviews for, (2) submitted an article to, (3) written a book or media review for, or (4) taken on the editorship of a scholarly journal published by giant firms such as Springer, Reed Elsevier, or Wiley, then you belong to a very large group of very well-educated people whose unpaid labor has helped make these firms very profitable. In turn, their profitability has positioned them to work vigorously against the interests of (1) university presses and other nonprofit publishers in the public interest, (2) libraries at all levels, (3) university and college students, (4) scholars themselves, and (5) particular and general publics with a need to consult the scholarly record.

I am not willing to freely give my labor to large multinational corporations whose interests align with their shareholders, but are antagonistic to my own. This is my view on one key aspect of scholarly communication today. Scholars can advance several different worthwhile causes by doing all that they can to stop becoming further entangled (individually and collectively) with for-profit scholarly publishers—particularly, the largest of the multinational firms that increasingly seek to exert a kind of hegemony over the entire domain of scholarly communication.

There is a great variety of steps that can be taken to build a different, more accessible, and progressive system of scholarly communication. My focus here is on five simple choices that scholars can make while sitting at their desks pursuing their own publishing work. These are choices that I have made and that I encourage my colleagues to consider making.

1. Choose not to submit scholarly journal articles or other works to publications owned by for-profit firms.

2. Say no, when asked to undertake peer-review work on a book or article manuscript that has been submitted for publication by a for-profit publisher, or a journal under the control of a commercial publisher.
3. Do not seek or accept the editorship of a journal owned or under the control of a commercial publisher.
4. Do not take on the role of series editor for a book series being published by a for-profit publisher.
5. Turn down invitations to join the editorial boards of commercially published journals or book series.

If taken, the preceding steps are individual in their point of action, even as they support a variety of more collective projects aimed at redirecting the scholarly communication system in more progressive, sustainable, and open ways.

If you care about university presses, these steps will help. If you are eager to resist corporate enclosure of public goods, resources, and ideas, they will help. If you care about reform in intellectual property systems, they will help. If you are worried that your college or university library is on the brink of financial collapse, they will help. If you want to make sure that your scholarship is as available as possible to colleagues, students, and the public, they will help. If you believe in open education and other approaches to transforming teaching and learning, they will help. If you are concerned about the harmful effects of media consolidation, they will help. If you are selfish and resent being taken advantage of, they will help.

What choices are you making? Are you ready to get out of the business?

Burn the Boats/Books

David Parry

When Marc Andreesen, the entrepreneur behind the first mainstream web browser, was interviewed by the popular technology blog, *TechCrunch*, on the future of publishing—in particular, journalism—his provocative response was "burn the boats." What he was referring to was the moment Cortez, fleeing from Cuba, and landing in Mexico, ordered his troops to "burn the boats," preventing any possibility of return. The lesson: don't defend lost ground; at times there is no going back; making decisions to insure that one does not consider a return is a good move. Andreesen's point was that old print-based media forms are dead, and it does no good to try and reenvision them for the twenty-first century. Rather, journalism institutions need to boldly move to future web-based models, giving up on their print-based biases.[1]

Academics should similarly "burn their boats," or in this case, "burn the books," making a definitive move to embrace new modes of scholarships enabled by web-based communication, rather than attempting to port old models into the new register. Rather than providing the book with a digital facelift for twenty-first-century scholarly communication, academics should move past book-based biases—which structure scholarly communications, and instead imagine and execute digitally born scholarly forms—which leverage the evolving digital-media landscape.

This is not to suggest that we actually engage in book burning. Instead, we need to burn our love affair with books, and that out of reverence to the book, we stop treating it as the only, or even primary, means of scholarly communication. Not only are there better ways, but if academia wants to remain—or more skeptically, become—relevant, we ought to recognize that the book is no longer the main mode of knowledge transmission.

Faced with the transformation to a digital format, the newspaper industry chose to protect a business model, instead of preserving their social function. My fear is that academics are making the same mistake. Granted, this analogy is not perfect—there are contours and shapes, and nuance and details that matter here. They are not a direct equivalence, but the underlying logic is the same. It concerns me that academics and intellectuals, with some exceptions, seem to be repeating this mistake, following the digital facelift model, asking how they can continue to do what they do now, but do it in the digital space, rather than asking how what they do has been fundamentally changed in the age of the digital networked archive.

It is worth distinguishing here between the materiality of the book, and the ideologies and biases we associate with the book. At the most basic level, a book is a dead tree processed and bound together in leaves of paper and stained with ink. But many of the things that we have come to associate with the book are not in fact coterminous with its material structure, but rather biases developed over the "Gutenberg Parenthesis," the relatively brief period in human history when print was the dominant form of communication, following a long oral period, and now succeeded by a digital age that has much in common with preprint culture.

This librocentricism—or a book-biased way of thinking, where the book stands in for certain prejudices and ideas about knowledge—is pervasive. Notice how the word "book" often stands in for, or comes to mean, the entirety of the matter, as in *The Book of Nature,* to "throw the book at someone," or "The Book of Love." So often "book" comes to be an epistemological framework for knowledge, not just a material one.

The idea that knowledge is a product, which can be delivered in an analog vehicle, needs to be questioned. What the network shows us is that many of our views of information were/are based on librocentric biases. While the book treats information as something scarce, the Net shows us precisely the opposite—information is anything but scarce. Books tell us that one learns by acquiring information, something which is purchased and traded as a commodity, consumed and mastered, but the Net shows us that knowledge is actually about navigating, creating, participating.

Knowledge is no longer print-based, nor governed by the substrate of paper; indeed, while in many ways we might continue to harbor librocentric biases, as we move away from structuring knowledge to end up on paper, these framing structures will prove less and less necessary; indeed, may actually impede on our ability to participate in knowledge conversations.

We do not have to give up completely on books, freeing ourselves from all of the pages we have in our respective offices. Rather, we should start conceiving of our scholarship as if it will not end up in books—indeed it still might—but begin by asking ourselves what would scholarship look like if it were not designed to end up in books.

Here are some suggestions for this change:

Stop publishing in closed systems. If you publish in a journal that charges for access, you are not published, you are private-ed. To publish means to make public; if something is locked down behind a firewall where someone needs a subscription to view it, it is not part of the common knowledge base and thus might as well not exist. Academic journals are treating knowledge as if it is a scarce commodity: it is not; do not let them treat it as such. If someone wants to publish something you wrote, ask them if you can keep the copyright and license it under Creative Commons, and if they say no, do not give it to them, and find someone who will. Look for journals that publish only online, and only for free.

Self-publish. Publishing and editing are hacks based on the scarcity of paper; no need to carry it over to the new medium. Once, print-based publishing was the most efficient way to reach the largest audience. That is no longer the case, so let's get over our print-based publishing fetish. Publishing online allows you to engage a wider audience—faster, and more efficiently than any print-based journal. We think of an academic's role as presenting polished finished work and ideas, but this need not be the case. We should switch to presenting our ideas in process, showing our work—not just the final product.

Digital publications must interact with the web. A PDF document is not a web-based document. It is a print-based document distributed on the web. One of the principal advantages of the web is the way it connects, and operates as a network of connections within an ecosystem of knowledge where one can search, copy, paste, edit, and link with ease—none of which is true of a PDF. The PDF is just a way of maintaining print-based aesthetics and structures on the web. In the same way you wouldn't think of publishing a book without the appropriate footnotes, don't publish to the web without the appropriate live links.

Get over peer review. Peer review is another hack based on the scarcity of paper. Given the cost of producing knowledge, and the fact that academic journals or academic presses could only afford to produce so many pages with each journal, peers are established to vet, and to signal that a particular piece is credible and more worthy than others. This is the filter-then-publish model. But the Net actually works in reverse—publish then filter—involving a wider range of people in the discursive production. Why do academics argue for small-panel, anonymous peer review? One thing we know is that diversity of perspective enriches discourse.

Aspire to be a curator. We have to give up being authorities, controlling our discourse, and seeing ourselves as experts who possess bodies of knowledge over which we have mastery. Instead, we have to start thinking of what we do as participating in a conversation—an ongoing process of knowledge formation. What if we thought of academics as curators—people who keep things up to date, clean, host, point, and aggregate knowledge, rather than just those who are responsible for producing new knowledge. Do we really need another book arguing that throughout the history of literary scholarship the important field of "x" has long been ignored? No. But we could actually use some good online resources and aggregators for particular subject domains.

Think beyond the book. Think of the book as one form, not *the* form. Indeed, think of things that move beyond the book. What if what you are writing didn't have to be stable, didn't have to have a final version? What if you could constantly update, alter, and make available your work? There will be no final copy, just the most recent version. While the constantly-in-beta mode might concern those who aim for perfection, it can also be liberating when you realize that nothing is fixed, taking advantage of the fluidity of the Net. What happens when we give up on, or at least refuse to be limited by, librocentricism? What if a piece didn't have to be 20 pages for a journal article, or 250 for a book? There are economic constraints that place limits on the size and shape of academic writing—how much better can we be when we get rid of these? What would an academic argument as an app look like?

To be clear: the book isn't dead, but it is no longer central. Academia would do well to recognize this; to move into new directions, new grounds, where many already are. We should not continue to constrain our thinking by a librocentricism which no longer structures or limits the way that knowledge is produced, disseminated, or archived.

Note

1. Erick Schonfeld, "Andreessen's Advice to Old Media: 'Burn The Boats,'" *TechCrunch*, March 6, 2010, http://techcrunch.com/2010/03/06/andreessen-media-burn-boats/.

Reinventing the Academic Journal

Jo Guldi

The web is thirsty for efficient, effective ways of retrieving useful information about the state of the field. This pressure creates an enormous market for those instruments that help individuals locate authoritative discourses and situated scholarship, and this, of course, is one of the traditional roles of the academic journal.

Academic journals are in the course of rethinking their management, methods, and publication standards. If they face this transition with courage and ingenuity, journals have the opportunity to plant themselves firmly as pillars of professional utility, scholarly collaboration, and authoritative knowledge as a public utility. Much of it may require thinking in terms of shifting communities and the life of information, and shifting sharply away from current journals' dependence on issue-by-issue websites and PDF servers like JSTOR. If you're a journal editor, the first step in a shift away may indeed be so radical as taking down your website, sharing information in new ways even more deeply integrated with the flow of information on Web 2.0.

There are four major ways to adapt academic publication to a Web 2.0 world.

1) Journals must pursue interoperability with the other online tools that are shaping the techne of scholarly practice.

Web 2.0 requires public visibility and interoperability with other web tools, in order that a searching aid should be found, adopted, and rendered relevant to the new research paradigms being adopted by scholars and members of the public alike. The more journals fit themselves into this paradigm, the better they'll thrive in the new order, finding readers both academic and paraacademic as allies. They will function usefully as finding aids for the most relevant, expert material in their disciplines.

In going Web 2.0, journals have the ability to mesh their publications with tools that will allow readers to better integrate journal essays with the rest of their research. A scholar using a research manager like Zotero and JSTOR currently can download the article PDF and the citation, ready for use in a footnote. Web 2.0 journals must go further into this zone: a scholar using Zotero, JSTOR, Google Scholar, and a social bookmarking tool can instantaneously find other scholars' opinions of a particular article, the names of the disciplines and subdisciplines they think it best applies to, and other articles of similar note to that particular scholar.

With these tools, every published article becomes easily interfaced with the tools new scholars are using to sort their data. Each visitor to a Web 2.0 service can refashion their own reading list from their colleagues' reading lists—cutting and pasting collective knowledge into an individual canon suited to their own project.

2) Journals have opportunity to reframe their role in the academy as curators of the noise of the web.

The web suffers from a crisis of authority, which is being met on the individual, rather than the collective and disciplinary level. For questions of disciplinary fields, for example, *Wikipedia* is likely to be irrelevant and useless. Far more useful, from my point of view, have been peer-to-peer exchanges on social-bookmarking and -networking sites like Delicious, LibraryThing, and Twitter, where colleagues in proximate fields have openly shared their course reading material, current research, and private canons.

On these sharing sites, individuals tag interesting citations with a series of terms most relevantly useful to their own practice. Users are less concerned with the interoperability of those selected terms than with the project of generating as many accurate, natural-language keywords as possible (folksonomy). The collected mass of these tags becomes an ultimate subject catalog to all the possible subject headings that might apply to any given website. Particular individual users become sources of authority for a given subject heading.

Journals have the opportunity to weave themselves as crucial threads in the fabric of online conversations if they begin tagging, becoming collective repositories of the best, collectively ratified articles and citations available for download on the web.

In a world where the primary tools for finding new scholarship are tagged, social databases like Delicious and LibraryThing, the most efficient form of journal interface with the world might be for journals to scrap their websites and become collective, tagging entities. In the world of the traditional print journal, scholars vied to get a *Journal of Modern History* citation on their curriculum vitae because it stands for something. What if instead there was a filtered set of citations produced by those entities?

Such a stream of official citations could come to stand in for the private account of a collective recognized for setting a standard in the field, providing much the same function as the old print citation in terms of scholarly participation and professional standing.

Being collected in those entries could still stand for the product of collective vetting among recognized scholars.

Web 2.0 journals that take their primary responsibility as curatorial have no need for official publication from the university-press system. They are not dependent on the income model of the university press, and they have no reason to collect subscriptions: their purpose is disciplinary service and public access. There is no reason for the articles published in this format to be made private, or to require elaborate fee-charging mechanisms.

3) Electronic journals will have the opportunity to expand their curatorial mandate to include different forms of publication.

The traditional journal collects and publishes only three sorts of essays: the editorial, the peer-reviewed essay of new research in fifteen–fifty pages, and the book review. There is nothing platonic about these forms: they evolved from the culture of eighteenth-century coffee-house journals, reviewing the books in circulation, and the canonization of eighteenth-century essayists like Addison and Steele in the English curriculum of higher education at the end of the nineteenth century. They are considered the template for developing a reasoned, supported argument, and so the metric for measuring the ability to research, argue, and write.

The traditional canon of essays, editorials, and book reviews has excluded much of other forms of scholarship, the circulation of whose best models are of value to the scholarly community, including: syllabi, subject-division lists for qualifying exams, lectures, paragraph-sized notes/queries, lists of relevant new electronic tools, reviews of electronic tools, reports on best methods in the archives, and blog-sized opinions about exciting new directions for the field. An electronic journal has no reason to exclude a twenty-minute audio segment, a selection of maps shared on SlideShare, or a video segment of a conference paper shared on YouTube. Properly curated, any of these categories would be of immense disciplinary interest, worthy of collection in a journal stream.

4) Against exclusive publication.

It is contrary to utility, in the world of Web 2.0, to maintain exclusive publication rights on an article. Exclusivity of publication places a text in only one domain. Yet nonexclusive text gets reproduced and recopied, circulated around the Internet, and rapidly floats onward to mimetic influence in other cultures, excerpted and referenced. For every Web 2.0 author, nonexclusivity and easy republication is ideal. For every would-be-idea-of-influence in the age of Web 2.0, easy reduplication is crucial.

Exclusivity has been the format followed by most online journals, which seek to mimic in form the traditional journal: one essay, neatly formatted, looking as professional as possible. Exclusive republication suggests the old model of authority, and is superficially reassuring to editors without actually promoting the real functions of the journal: disseminating ideas and establishing the authority of the journal-as-canon and disciplinary metric.

Significantly more desirable would be setting a different precedent: for all disseminated forms of the text to advertise the article's accreditation as having been curated by inclusion in the journal-as-stream. If this dissemination model is followed, the journal home page need not include reprints of the articles themselves: merely links to the original blogspace or university-housed PDF or slideshow where the material was originally posted, with all of its links, illustrations, video, and wallpaper as the author originally presented it. The journal's role is reduced to curation, not to presentation. Not having a use for a graphic designer, typesetter, or illustrations-layout person, the journal's workflow will be considerably reduced.

5) Broadening the criteria for participation.

Another major question opened by the age of the electronic journal is the issue of expertise. Like the essay, the journal peer-review process is the relic of another age: an age of abundant, unbegrudging emeriti with plentiful leisure to foster the development of younger peers who had, on average, three years of training by way of a PhD. The limited number of peer reviewers and editors responsible for the operation of the journal at any given time is the relic of the system limited by the expense of the post office, the limited social networks of the people who invented the system, and the era of fewer PhD's on the world scene. In a new era, many of the burdens of editing and curation can be more broadly distributed to both the aid of the editors and the thriving of the discipline itself.

Journals have the opportunity to reconsider the distribution of time and responsibility. Is peer review a top-down mentoring process for scaling up the academic ladder, or will it be reconceived as an open playing field—a sort of open seminar for peer review, rather than a two-vetted-readers-read-you system? With the aid of wikis and commenting systems, it becomes possible for a single text to be usefully reviewed and edited by hundreds of individuals—vetting their understanding of significance, authentic fact, and argument flow. For young scholars, accreted small suggestions of other citations, references, examples, and counterexamples, from a wider array of supporters, could conceivably enhance an article on multiple levels.

Additionally, the thinking of interdisciplinary members of the broader academy might be usefully invited. The pressure of other ideas could hypothetically encourage the discipline to take account of the findings of related subdisciplines (invited participation from scholars in postcolonial studies for *Victorian Studies* issues on empire), the concerns of related fields (are economists convinced by new findings in economic history?), and the legibility of argument to the public (does this groundbreaking, relevant article on tyranny and empire actually parse to the average reader of the *New York Times*?).

6) The reconsideration of timelines.

In the age of Web 2.0, it is also possible for a writer to continuously revise an argument over an extended period of time—even indefinitely. For the sake of scholars' multiple projects, an indefinitely revised work is probably not ideal, but extended revisions, over the course of a year, become possible and useful for the author and the discipline. An article could be published as "officially under review" in a subcategory of the journal stream, subjected to gradual wiki conversation for a year, and remain available to a reading public for the entirety of that time.

The product that would emerge at the end of a year of wiki-ratification would be very different than that at the beginning. If the author failed, in the course of wiki revision, to produce a stronger article than at the beginning, the article could be removed from the journal stream at the end of the year.

Reading and Writing

Michael O'Malley

The way we're taught to read is diametrically opposite the way we're taught to write. We learn to read books and articles quickly, under pressure, for the key points or for what we can use. But we write as if a learned gentleman of leisure sits in a paneled study, savoring every word. Books and articles are clogged with prose no one but first-year graduate students and the author's most devoted enemies actually read. Yet the titles of books and articles suggest the author imagines a literary audience of breathless millions. *An Age of Giants: Railroad Regulation in Kansas, 1933–1936*. Did I make this title up? Hard to tell, isn't it? Why do sober, solid academic tomes feel obliged to tart up their work like middle-aged trollops?

It's because of the disjunction between the way we are taught to read and the way we are taught to write. We aspire to write in what might be called, if one were feeling extremely generous, a "literary" style. But we learn to read as if gutting a fish. The state of affairs is well described by a joke many have heard or told:

Professor A: "Have you taught this new book by X?" Professor B: "Why not only have I taught it, I've read it!"

Within these comically unrealistic parameters, academic writing finds an extremely limited set of outlets. There are books, there are journal articles, and there are conference papers, which are but fetal journal articles or book chapters. Scholarly books and articles are, quite reasonably, hard to publish. They need peer review, which takes time; at its best, peer review makes for better, more reliable, more accurate work. At its worst, it wears interesting and novel ideas down to a smooth, dull, and uniform familiarity. It demands exactly the narcotizing qualifications and historiographic forced marches that put ordinary readers off academic work and render the colonic titles absurd.

When you think back on the books and articles that most influenced you, is your first thought "hell of a job on the peer review"? The stuff which has been most influential in my intellectual life, the stuff that's been most profound and useful, is profound and useful in ways that have nothing at all to do with peer review.

Was Foucault's *Discipline and Punish* peer reviewed? It sure doesn't read as if it was. *History of Sexuality*, Volume 1? No. Both books had a profound influence. Was Geertz's essay on cockfighting in Bali dramatically improved by peer review? No. What's valuable about that famous essay is the clarity of his prose and the nature of the insights. Maybe peer review pushed him to make it a little better, but the value comes from the method, the intellectual core, not some fine-tuning on Balinese village customs forced by Geertz's disciplinary rivals.

Now the obvious objection is that peer review is supposed to be invisible, and present us—the general public—with a reliable, vetted, accurate product. One could argue that in these examples, it worked as it was supposed to. But again it's not the fact that they were peer-reviewed that makes these pieces worthwhile: peer review is to their worth as the parsley garnish is to the blue-plate special.

Now, of course, most of us are not brilliant thinkers, and even brilliant thinkers get help. No doubt Geertz, Foucault, and other postmodern worthies worked in a community, and benefited from exchange with their peers. We all want that input on our work: we want to clarify our thinking and gain from the insights of people we respect. But in a networked world there are ways to make that easier, not harder: more fluid and less cumbersome.

And because there are so very few templates for academic publishing, scholars have to inflate their work to fit—the book is all too often a blown-up article, and the article, all too often, is a blown-up conference paper. Does anyone doubt this? There's no outlet for small ideas, for what the sciences call a "research finding." There are few outlets for work that frankly mixes past history with present politics. There are few or no outlets for work that takes chances with form. It's as if basketball was still played only by slow midwestern men lobbing set shots.

Academic writing has been remarkably resistant to technological change. It survived the typewriter crisis with nary a blip; the word processor, despite its immense advantages, left little or no mark on academic prose, except that really good quotations tended to be repeated more often. So it continues today, blithely untouched by the staggering potential of networked digital technology, writing as if a neighbor had just dropped by in a carriage and left their card in the foyer. Yes, methodologies change;

the liquid in the glass changes colors and flavors, but the glass remains thick, square, and clouded with age.

There is of course nothing intrinsically wrong with the current model of academic publishing, just as there's nothing wrong with Brahms. But a world in which Brahms was the only template for musical expression would be both stupefying and willfully cloistered. Why not invent a new mode of academic publishing and communication—one rooted in the way we actually live and work; one that takes advantage of the technologies we have, instead of pretending they don't exist?

Voices

BLOGGING

Matthew G. Kirschenbaum, Mark Sample, Daniel J. Cohen

The science fiction writer Harlan Ellison once described a stunt in which he sat in the window of a bookshop all day, writing a story. He was curious about what would happen if writing became a public spectacle rather than the mysterious, solitary endeavor it usually is. That scene piqued my imagination and stuck with me, enough so that when I explored the idea of writing an electronic dissertation in the mid-1990s—at the same time the web was emerging as a popular medium but before the term "blog" had been coined—I immediately decided do it it live, in real time, on the network; that is, I would simply publish drafts of my work, revise them, and the whole would take shape as a massive, interlaced hypertext. The idea was to keep myself motivated. By writing in a fishbowl, I reasoned, I would have some real, external pressure to keep at it. I would never know who was reading (watching). Yes, the fishbowl was also a panopticon. Was I worried about plagiarism when I published drafts of my dissertation online? Nope—red herring. I was branding my ideas, imprinting them with my name, and putting them into public circulation. Sure enough, there followed conference invitations, citations of my work in other scholars' work, and contacts and connections that to this day form the basis of my professional community. What I really wanted, of course, was a blog.

—MATTHEW G. KIRSCHENBAUM

I don't expect my blog to affect my career one way or another. It's not like I'm spreading gossip, sharing dark fantasies, or posting my neuroses. Many of my posts are simply observations—the kind I would talk about with a group of friends, if I still had the time. But I'm too busy teaching and writing to sit around anymore and talk about these kinds of things. So I steal a few random minutes, spit them out on my blog, and then I forget about them. The posts that aren't simply observations are usually ideas in incubation that will eventually surface—peer-reviewed, documented, cited, bleached of personality—in a conference paper, journal article, or someday, a book. The posts are placeholders, in a sense, for the real intellectual work that lies ahead.

—MARK SAMPLE

When I was in graduate school, a mentor once told me that the key to being a successful scholar was to become completely obsessed with a historical topic, to feel the urge to read and learn everything about an event, an era, or a person—in short, to become so knowledgeable, energetic, and even obsessed with your subject matter that you become what others immediately recognize as a trusted, valuable expert. The most stimulating, influential professors, even those with more traditional outlets for their work—like books and journals—overflow with views and thoughts. As it turns out, blogs are perfect outlets for obsession. Shaped correctly, a blog can be a perfect place for that extra production of words and ideas. The best bloggers inevitably become a nexus for information exchange in their field.

—DANIEL J. COHEN

The Crisis of Audience and the Open-Access Solution

John Unsworth

When my daughter Eleanor, now twenty-one, was about three years old, she had an imaginary friend. One day I asked her friend's name. "Audience," she said. Today, Eleanor has real friends; it's the humanities scholar who has an imaginary audience.

We hear often, these days, of a crisis in scholarly publishing, usually attributed to the rise in the cost of science, technical, and medical serials, the decline in library budgets, and the resulting squeeze on standing orders for university-press monographs. But there is another, more direct, explanation for the difficulty that university presses are having in publishing humanities monographs. The simplest analysis of the "crisis in scholarly publishing" is that it's a problem of audience: nobody's reading these books—not even colleagues in the disciplines, much less students, or the general public.

There are a number of possible readings of this crisis of audience: I'd like to consider them one by one, and consider how open access might make a difference—or not—in each case. I realize that open access is usually discussed in connection with journal literature, and I will return to the question of journals later on, but for now, I'll be looking at monographs—single-author, book-length works of scholarship—in the humanities.

Reading 1. The problem is that humanities scholarship is too full of jargon—it is intentionally obscure.

This is a plausible analysis, on its face, and it's one you will often hear from humanities scholars themselves, when they are speaking of the work of others. Speaking as the editor emeritus of a humanities journal that, in one issue, published "'The Feathery Rilke Mustaches and Porky Pig Tattoos on Stomach': High and Low Pressures in Gravity's Rainbow," and "'Mais ce n'est surtout pas vrai': On Some Recent Re-Citings of Jacques Derrida," and "Currency Exchanges: The Postmodern, Vattimo, Et Cetera, Among Other Things (Et Cetera)," I believe there is some basis for the charge of obscurantism.

If this is the whole story, then open access won't make a bit of difference: nobody will be interested, and the material won't be any more accessible, just because the scholarship is available for free. On the other hand, it won't do any harm, because the market for the books is not one that will evaporate if the same content is available for free: individuals aren't buying these books, and a library that collects them does so in order to build a collection, for use in the future as well as the present. The availability of the content online is a present convenience, but its future is, at best, uncertain.

The counterargument to the obscurantism analysis, though, is that it sells both the scholarship and the audience short. Granted, the United States has never been kind to highbrow cultural production, in any era or medium, and while we sometimes lament the low level of mass media, as a nation we definitely—sometimes defiantly—prefer Porky Pig to Rilke. And yet, during the period—about fourteen years ago—when this issue of *Postmodern Culture* came out, the journal—freely available on the web—was receiving upward of a million hits a year, and during that same period, I received this email from a reader:

> Dear Mr. Unsworth: I'm a union teamster living in rural Vermont so I don't have a lot of access to the sort of stuff you have in your journal and you provide access to from your Web site. Our local library is swell, computerized too, but a computer search under postmodernism or poststructuralism or Derrida or Baudrillard or Jameson produces zero hits. Thank you.

I'll come back to this point, but for now, I'll just say that the world is full of surprises, and one of them may be that there's an audience for scholarship outside the academy, and if that audience isn't imaginary, then open-access publishing would be the best way to reach them. Of course, adding open-access publishing to print publishing has a cost, so if the print enterprise is already not viable, and the open-access audience doesn't exist, gambling on open access and losing may hasten the slow, but apparently inevitable, decline of the humanities monograph. I'd there's still nothing to lose: if this mode of scholarly communicati really not viable, it would be better for it to die off and be replace something new than to drag on, on life support, and stifle the potential emergence of new modes and genres of communication—possibly less obscure, more intellectually open-access ones, at that.

Reading 2. Esoteric publishing is just fine—but we don't need publishers to do it.

The notion of an "economics" of esoteric publishing, and indeed the phrase "esoteric publishing," belongs, so far as I know, to Stevan Harnad, the editor of *Psycoloquy*, and an electronic publisher who has been at it as long as I have. In Stevan's original proposition, called a "Subversive Proposal," he defined esoteric publishing as nontrade, no-market scientific and scholarly publication—the lion's share of the academic corpus and a body of work for which the author does not and never has expected to sell his words. He wants only to publish them; that is, to reach the eyes and minds of his peers, his fellow esoteric scientists and scholars the world over, so that they can build on one another's contributions in that cumulative, collaborative enterprise called learned inquiry. Stevan's subversive proposal is to argue that since scholars who publish for a specialized audience and have no expectation of being paid for their work can now publish cheaply on the Internet, therefore the publishers who formerly served this type of writer will have to either restructure themselves so as to arrange for the much-reduced electronic-only page costs, to be paid out of advance subsidies—from authors' page charges, learned-society dues, university publication budgets and/or governmental publication subsidies—or they will have to watch as the peer community spawns a brand-new generation of electronic-only publishers who will. The subversion will be complete, because the esoteric, no-market peer-reviewed literature will have taken to the airwaves, where it always belonged, and those airwaves will be free—to the benefit of us all—because their true minimal expenses will be covered the optimal way for the unimpeded flow of esoteric knowledge to all: in advance.

For truly esoteric publishing, Harnad's reasoning still holds. If the audience is very small, give it away: it's cheaper, all the way around. There may still be real costs to this sort of publishing, but—Stevan argues, and I agree—we'd be better off finding them from grants, subventions, or even page charges to authors, rather than playing the losing game of trying to recoup the costs of managing an editorial process on top of the costs of designing and manufacturing books, in a tiny and static market. In this case, again, open-access publishing makes sense: there are probably not many people who will want to read the stuff, but setting up toll barriers to access will probably cost more to administer than it will bring in, and the scholars themselves are motivated by audience, so even a modest increase in readership, through free access and electronic distribution, increases the author's motivation—perhaps enough to per-page-fees, if that's necessary.

Reading 3. Get a bigger audience.

The third possible response to the crisis of audience is that humanities scholarship needs to get a bigger audience. On that subject, in a talk given at the 2003 annual meeting of the American Council of Learned Societies, I suggested that we could enlarge the audience for humanities scholarship, not by dumbing it down, but by making it more readily available. Maybe if we did that, scholars would find an audience first, and a publisher second, instead of the other way around. Maybe in that world, too, the risk to publishers would decrease, because the demand would already be demonstrated. I am constantly surprised, frankly, at how little faith humanities scholars, and their publishers, have in the audience appeal of humanities scholarship. This lack of faith is attributable in part to self-loathing, in part to lack of respect for the general public, and in part to disappointing sales figures, of course—but the net effect is stifling. If this analysis is correct, open access could make a big difference—but you have to believe that the audience is out there. Now, I recognize that the general public isn't browsing the catalogs of university presses, nor stopping in to their nearest research library—but they are on the web, and they are looking for information on a very wide range of subjects, as my rusticated unionized postmodernist demonstrates. Techniques of predicting taste, such as collaborative filtering, could also expose niche audiences difficult to find in other ways, but still large enough to be significant. If there's even a few hundred of these people out there, in any given subject area, and if they even occasionally want to buy the book version of something they've read online, then perhaps it would make sense to provide open access to everything, and then print, print on demand, or ebook those items that get heavily used. If you're worried about providing too close an equivalent for the print object, then make the content available as HTML, rather than

PDF—experiments at the National Academy Press have made it clear that free HTML does not cannibalize book sales, but actually (and markedly) increases them—and their front-page titles include things like "Damp Indoor Spaces and Health."

For heaven's sake: if the NAP can make this go, by providing open access to its content, how do you like the chances of a university press that publishes titles like *Hot Potato: How Washington and New York Gave Birth to Black Basketball and Changed America's Game Forever* (University of Virginia Press)?

So, if we accept that the crisis in scholarly publishing, in the humanities, is a crisis of audience, and if we accept these three possible responses to that crisis, then I would say open-access publishing is indicated, no matter what. In the first case, it can do no harm, except possibly hastening the demise of a doomed genre; in the second case, it can do a little good, at no added cost; in the third case, it could do a great deal of good, by uncovering new audiences and reconnecting academic humanities with the reading public—and if experience in other apparently esoteric publishing enterprises like the National Academies holds true, it might reverse the fortunes of the university presses at the same time.

Open-Access Publishing

Kathleen Fitzpatrick

Raising the idea of open-access publishing among contemporary scholars produces an immediate and sometimes surprising set of responses—ranging from enthusiasm, to anger, to befuddlement. The open-access movement has a wide range of proponents and an often-entrenched opposition, and the depth of feeling on both sides often leaves those scholars in between scratching their heads, wondering exactly what the deal is.

A huge part of the confusion arises from the proliferation of misinformation and mythology around the notion of open access; opponents of open access alternately argue that making all scholarship available for free will destroy the economic model of the publishing industry, making it impossible for anything to get published, and that doing so will simultaneously undermine peer review, turning all scholarship into vanity publishing, allowing anything to get published. Neither of these things is true; open-access publishing does not necessarily mean making everything available free of cost, nor does it necessarily imply the absence of peer-review processes. It doesn't mean that scholars lose control of the copyright of their publications—from a certain perspective, we've long since given that away, but that's a matter for another time—and it doesn't mean that plagiarism will become more prevalent.

The open-access movement in contemporary scholarship began in large part with the sciences, as a response to the predatory practices of certain commercial journal publishers. By the early 1990s, a small number of large commercial publishers had acquired most of the top journals in many fields and had begun developing a range of profit-oriented pricing structures, including bundling together large groups of journals to which libraries are required to subscribe in order to gain access to the key journals that they actually want. Because of these practices, many less affluent institutions in the United States—much less those institutions in developing nations—have become unable to afford to provide access to the most important research being done in the STEM fields (science, technology, engineering, and mathematics). And, of course, scholars without official ties to a subscribing institution, including independent researchers and un- and under-employed faculty members, are often unable to access that scholarship as well.

Scholars in the humanities should of course be held to the same ethical obligations as those in the sciences; though the products of our research may not always appear to be as crucial to the health and well-being of diverse populations, our work nonetheless has potentially profound implications for popular discussions about the politics of cultural representations, about the meaning of human interactions, and so forth.

We in the humanities often resist opening our work to the broader public, fearing the consequences of such openness—and not without reason. The public at times fails to understand our work, and, because the content of the work seems as though it ought to be comprehensible (you're just writing about books, or movies, or art, after all!), isn't inclined to wrestle with the difficulties that our work presents; their dismissive responses give us the clear sense that the public doesn't take our work as seriously as, say, papers in high-energy physics, which few lay readers would assume the ability to comprehend without some background or training. As a result of this double misunderstanding, we close our work off from the public, arguing that we're only writing for a small group of specialists anyhow. In that case, why would open access matter?

The problem, of course, is that the more we close our work away from the public, and the more we refuse to engage in dialogue with them, the more we undermine that public's willingness to fund our research and our institutions. Closing our work away from the public, and keeping our scholarly conversations private, might protect us from public criticism, but it can't protect us from public apathy—a condition that is, in the current economy, far more dangerous. This is not to say that such openness doesn't bear risks, particularly for scholars working in controversial areas of research, but it is to say that only through open dialogue across the walls of the ivory tower will we have any chance of convincing the broader public, including our governmental funding bodies, of the importance of our work.

Few may know that many journals in the humanities have published in a free and open fashion since the early days of the web; the *Electronic Book Review*, for instance, was founded in 1994, and has been in continuous, open publication since. *Kairos*, likewise, has been in open, online publication since 1996. Open Humanities Press publishes a range of open-access, peer-reviewed journals online.[1] Journals such as these generally operate on very limited budgets, cobbling together a range of support, including grants from funding bodies and staff/in-kind support from the journal's host institution. But much of the support that such journals rely upon is volunteer labor—unpaid editors and reviewers, volunteer designers and coders, and so forth. This situation isn't all that different from more traditional, publisher-based models of journal production; whether the end result is distributed by commercial or university presses, the support that those entities provide to a journal's editors is generally slim at best. Economist Theodore C. Bergstrom argued this point in his 2001 paper, "Free Labor for Costly Journals?," advocating that scholars refuse to publish in overpriced commercial journals.[2]

A more radical reason for espousing open-access publishing, however, is to reclaim the value of our labor for the profession itself. It isn't just ethically incumbent on us as scholars to *publish* in open-access venues, but in fact to *create* more open-access publications, and more systems for their support. These systems might include new public or foundation-based granting agency programs specifically designed to support open-access publications. They might include more consortial agreements among universities to create and support open-access publications.[3] They might include the development of new tools to assist in the labor that goes into journal production, such as the Public Knowledge Project's open-source project, Open Journal Systems, which helps to create a workflow that reduces a journal editor's reliance on technical personnel and expensive web production.

The key point, though, is that we need to take back our publications from the market-based economy, and to reorient scholarly communication within the gift economy that best enables our work to thrive. We are, after all, already doing the labor for free—the labor of research, the labor of writing, the labor of editing—as a means of contributing to the advancement of the collective knowledge in our fields. We should value our labor sufficiently to ensure that we, our institutions, our colleagues, and our students have full and perpetual access to the results of our work—and promoting the development of open-access publishing venues, and contributing all of our work to them, are the best ways to meet that ethical imperative toward the widest possible distribution of the knowledge that we produce.

Notes

1. "Electronic Book Review," http://www.electronicbookreview.com/. "Kairos: A Journal of Rhetoric, Technology, and Pedagogy," http://kairos.technorhetoric.net/. "Open Humanities Press," http://openhumanitiespress.org/.

2. Theodore Bergstrom, "Free Labor for Costly Journals?," March 20, 2001, http://www.econ.ucsb.edu/%7Etedb/jep.pdf.

3. "Compact for OA Publishing Equity," http://www.oacompact.org/.

Open Access and Scholarly Values

A CONVERSATION

Daniel J. Cohen, Stephen Ramsay, Kathleen Fitzpatrick

Open-Access Publishing and Scholarly Values (Part 1)

—Daniel J. Cohen

There is a supply side and a demand side to scholarly communication. The supply side is the creation of scholarly works, including writing, peer review, editing, and the form of publication. The demand side is much more elusive—the mental state of the audience that leads them to "buy" what the supply side has produced. In order for the social contract to work, for engaged reading to happen, and for credit to be given to the author—or editor of a scholarly collection—both sides need to be aligned properly.

How can we increase the supply of open-access scholarship and prod scholars to be more receptive to scholarship that takes place outside of the traditional publishing system? One way is to appeal to four core scholarly values and emotions.

1. Impartiality

In my second year in college I had one of those late-night discussions where half-baked thoughts are exchanged, and everyone tries to impress each other with how smart and hip they are—a sophomoric gabfest, literally and figuratively. The conversation inevitably turned to music. I reeled off the names of bands I thought would get me the most respect. Another, far more mature student then said something that caught everyone off guard, paraphrasing Duke Ellington: "Well, to be honest, I just like *good* music." We all laughed—and then realized how true that statement was.

And secretly, we all did like a wide variety of music—from rock, to bluegrass, to big-band jazz.

Upon reflection, many of the best things we discover in scholarship—and life—are found in this way: by disregarding popularity and packaging and approaching creative works without prejudice. We wouldn't think much of *Moby-Dick* if Carl Van Doren hadn't looked past decades of mixed reviews to find the genius in Melville's writing. Art historians have similarly unearthed talented artists who did their work outside of the royal academies or art schools. As the unpretentious wine writer Alexis Lichine shrewdly said in the face of fancy labels and appeals to mythical "terroir": "There is no substitute for pulling corks."

Writing is writing and good is good, no matter the venue of publication or what the crowd thinks. Scholars surely understand that on a deep level, yet many persist in valuing venue and medium over the content itself. This is especially true at crucial moments, such as promotion and tenure. Surely we can reorient ourselves to our true core value—to honor creativity and quality—which will still guide us to many traditionally published works, but will also allow us to consider works in some nontraditional venues such as new open-access journals, blogs, articles written and posted on a personal website or institutional repository, or nonnarrative digital projects.

2. Passion

Do you get up in the morning wondering what journal you're going to publish in next, or how you're going to spend your ten-dollar royalty check? No. We wake up with ideas swirling around inside our head about the topic we're currently thinking about, and the act of writing is a way to satisfy our obsession and communicate our ideas to others. Being a scholar is an affliction of which scholarship is a symptom. If you're publishing primarily for careerist reasons and don't deeply care about your subject matter, I recommend you find another career.

The entire commercial apparatus of the existing publishing system takes advantage of our scholarly passion and the writing that passion inevitably creates. The system is far from perfect for maximizing the spread of our ideas, not to mention the economic bind it has put upon our institutions. If you were designing a system of scholarly communication today, in the age of the web, would it look like the one we have today? Disparage bloggers all you like, but they control their communication platform and the outlet for their passion, and most scholars and academic institutions don't.

3. Shame

In the spring of 2010, ITHAKA—the nonprofit that runs JSTOR and that has a research wing to study the transition of academia into the digital age—put out a report, "Key Insights for Libraries, Publishers, and Societies," based on a survey of faculty in 2009.[1] The report has two major conclusions. First, scholars are increasingly using online resources like Google Books as a starting point for their research rather than the physical library; that is, they have become comfortable with certain aspects of "going digital."

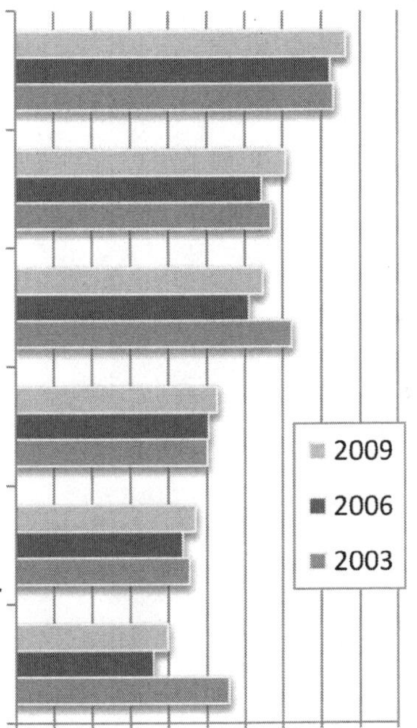

Figure 23 from ITHAKA: "Faculty Survey 2009: Key Strategic Insights for Libraries, Publishers, and Societies." Roger C. Schonfeld (manager of research) and Ross Housewright (analyst). http://www.ithaka.org/ithaka-s-r/research/faculty-surveys-2000-2009/faculty-survey-2009.

At the same time, though, the ITHAKA report notes that they remain stubbornly wedded to their old ways when it comes to using the digital realm for the composition and communication of their research. In other words, somehow it has become acceptable to use digital media and technology for parts of our work, but to resist it in others.

This divide is striking. The professoriate may be more liberal politically than the most latte-filled ZIP code in San Francisco, but we are an extraordinarily conservative bunch when it comes to scholarly communication. Look carefully at figure 23, above, a damning chart from the ITHAKA report.

Any faculty member who looks at this chart should feel ashamed. We professors care less about sharing our work—even with underprivileged nations that cannot afford access to gated resources—than with making sure we impress our colleagues; indeed, there was actually a sharp drop in professors who cared about open access between 2003 and 2009.

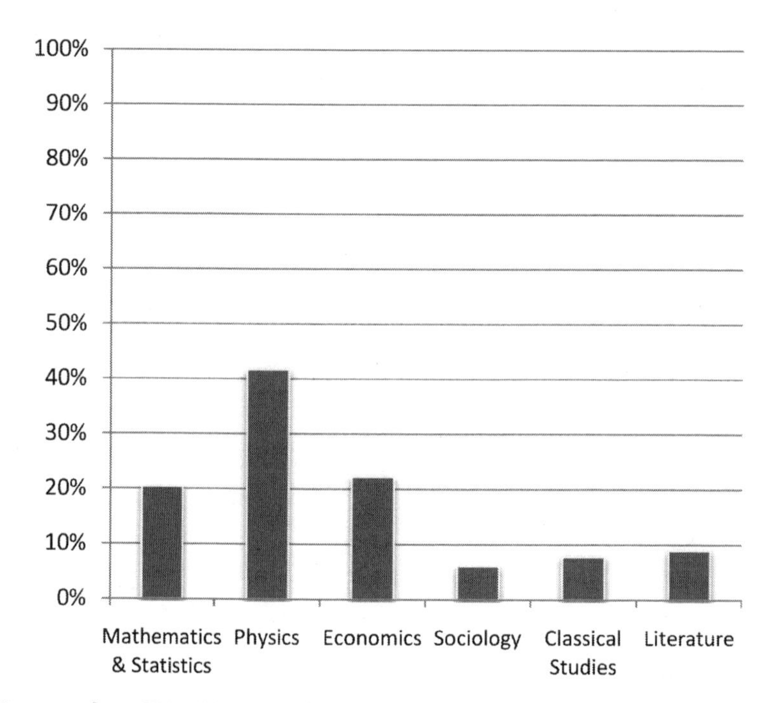

Figure 25 from ITHAKA: "Faculty Survey 2009: Key Strategic Insights for Libraries, Publishers, and Societies." Roger C. Schonfeld (manager of research) and Ross Housewright (analyst). http://www.ithaka.org/ithaka-s-r/research/faculty-surveys-2000-2009/faculty-survey-2009.

This would be acceptable if we understood ourselves to be ruthless, bottom-line-driven careerists. But that's not the caring educators we often pretend to be. Humanities scholars in particular have taken pride in the last few decades in uncovering and championing the voices of those who are less privileged and powerful, but here we are in the ivory tower, still preferring to publish in ways that separate our words from those of the online masses.

We can't even be bothered to share our old finished articles—already published, and our reputation suitably burnished—by putting them in an open institutional repository, as ITHAKA figure 25, above, makes clear.

Is there any other way to read these charts than as shameful hypocrisy?

4. Narcissism

The irony of this situation is that in the long run it very well may be better for the narcissistic professor in search of reputation to publish in open-access venues. When scholars do the cost-benefit analysis about where to publish, they frequently think about the reputation of the journal or press. That's the reason many scholars consider open access venues to be inferior, because they do not (yet) have the same reputation as the traditional closed-access publications.

Yet in their cost-benefit calculus they often forget to factor in the hidden costs of publishing in a closed way. The largest hidden cost is the invisibility of what you publish. When you publish somewhere that is behind gates, or in paper only, you are resigning all that hard work to invisibility in the age of the open web. You may reach a few peers in your field, but you miss out on the broader dissemination of your work, including to potential admirers.

The dirty little secret about open-access publishing is that while you may give up a line in your CV (although not necessarily), your work can be discovered much more easily by other scholars and interested parties, can be fully indexed by search engines, and can be linked to from other websites and social media (rather than leading to the dreaded "Sorry, this is behind a paywall" message).

When mathematician Grigori Perelman solved one of the greatest mathematical problems in history—the Poincaré conjecture—he didn't submit his solution to a traditional journal. He simply posted it to arXiv.org—an open-access website—and let others know about it. For him, just getting the knowledge out there was enough, and the mathematical community responded in kind by recognizing and applauding his work for what it was. Supply and demand intersected; scholarship was disseminated and credited without fuss over venue, and the results could be accessed by anyone with an Internet connection.

Is it so hard to imagine this as a more simple—and virtuous—model for the future of scholarly communication?

Open-Access Publishing and Scholarly Values (Part 2)
—*Stephen Ramsay*

"Writing is writing and good is good, no matter the venue of publication or what the crowd thinks. Scholars surely understand that on a deep level, yet many persist in valuing venue and medium over the content itself."

This is true, Dan. But it misses a key underlying reality of academic life: Few of the people who are actually responsible for evaluating your work actually read your books and articles.

That's probably an astounding revelation for many people who are coming up for tenure or who otherwise haven't had the opportunity to sit on a merit-review panel, but it's absolutely true. Your colleagues are not reading your work. Period.

How can this be? How can we make momentous decisions about promotion and tenure and conduct performance reviews that affect people's salaries without a comprehensive and thorough review of their work?

The answer is simple: publishers do it for us.

That's really what this is all about. We don't have time to read everything. But more importantly, we don't really want to evaluate our departmental colleagues' work on its "intellectual merits," because, well, they might in turn do that to us. And really, this could get very emotional, very quickly. And anyway, what qualifies us to judge one another? We're colleagues, after all.

The solution to everyone's problem has been to outsource this decision to a third party that gives it a seal of approval while at the same time anonymizing the people who actually read the book or article. That allows us to move the whole problem somewhere else. What's more, it allows us to make fine distinctions between people that we otherwise wouldn't want to make ourselves. The University of Chicago Press is better than Ashgate. Oxford is better than Michigan. *Critical Inquiry* is better than *Modern*

Drama. Monographs are better than edited collections. It's just so easy this way.

How does a profession that swings so solidly left hold such absurdly elitist attitudes? This apparent bit of cognitive dissonance is rooted in our mostly postmodern attitudes about value. "Who's to say what's good?" Humanities professors are mostly uncomfortable making judgments about what's good; publishers don't appear to have these deep philosophical problems (or rather, these philosophical issues are overridden by market concerns). There's also our desire to avoid confrontation ("Dude, that's so harsh"). Narcissism, sure. It's also full of contradictions. Why does Oxford University Press get to make truth claims about worth, but we don't? You could say that it's not actually the publishers; it's our "peers" on the anonymous review panels that the publishers hire.

But we pay a devastating price for that bit of bait and switch. First, it means that we have to sell our copyrights to compensate the publishers for their role in coordinating all of this. Since they're trying to stay afloat financially, they have to sell that content back to us—which usually results in highly restrictive forms of dissemination. Open access—which is an ethically superior form of dissemination on its face, and a moral obligation for public institutions—is effectively shut down by our own behavior. Second, it means that any form of scholarship not immediately susceptible to this treatment (e.g., the majority of digital work) can't participate equally in this system. Truth is, no one really has a problem anymore with digital work. It just has to be, you know, about article length. And single authored. And peer reviewed. And disseminated under the banner of a third party. And that's because this isn't about the medium at all. This is about the structures that allow us to make difficult decisions as painlessly as possible. I think most academics regard this as the best we can do.

This is not the best we can do. The idea of recording impact—page hits, links, etc.—is often ridiculed as a popularity contest, but it's not at all clear to me how such a system would be inferior to the one we have. In fact, it would almost certainly be a more honest system—you'll notice that "good publisher" is very often tied to the social class represented by the sponsoring institution. But in the end, the clear moral good of having open access—and the probable dissolution of the university-press system—may mean that we have to read and evaluate each other's work. That may mean that the mechanics of our entire review system has to change. It may actually mean that peer review, in its present form, disappears.

Those of us in the digital humanities have often wondered why our disciplines are so resistant to electronic publication, and digital projects in general. The standard answer "We don't know how to evaluate that kind of work," just doesn't make sense. Really?

Here's an idea: How about you look at it and decide whether it's good or not. But that's precisely the responsibility that no one wants to have. This is the root of every bit of sanctimonious nonsense you've ever heard about digital work not being peer-reviewed. Translation: We don't have a certifying authority to whom we can offload this.

Honestly, I think our goal as a community should be to present our colleagues with as many inscrutable objects as possible. We should be making lots of videos, podcasts, maps, "books" with a hundred authors, blog posts, software, and websites without any clear authorial control. And yes, we should put open-content licenses on all of it, and give it away to everyone we meet. We avoid efforts to create certifying authorities for digital work, which is simply capitulating to an already-broken system. Instead, we should dare our colleagues to engage our work and tell us that it isn't of sufficient intellectual quality.

Open-Access Publishing and Scholarly Values (Part 3)
—Kathleen Fitzpatrick

"The idea of recording impact—page hits, links, etc.—is often ridiculed as a popularity contest, but it's not at all clear to me how such a system would be inferior to the one we have. In fact, it would almost certainly be a more honest system—you'll notice that 'good publisher' is very often tied to the social class represented by the sponsoring institution."

Amen, Steve. At many institutions, the criteria for assessing a scholar's research for tenure and promotion include some statement about that scholar's "impact" on the field at a national or international level, and we treat the peer-review process as though it can give us information about such impact. But the fact of an article or a monograph's having been published by a reputable journal/press that employed the mechanisms of peer review as we currently know it—this can only ever give us binary information, and binary information based on an extraordinarily small sample size. Why should the two to three readers selected by a journal/press, plus that entity's editor/editorial board, be the arbiter of the authority of scholarly work—particularly in the digital realm, when we have so many more complex means of assessing the effect of/response to scholarly work via network analysis?

Going quantitative isn't the whole answer to our current problems with assessment in promotion and tenure reviews—our colleagues in the sciences would no doubt present us with all kinds of cautions about relying too exclusively on metrics like citation indexes and impact factor—but given that we in the digital humanities excel at both uncovering the networked relationships among texts, and at interpreting and articulating what those relationships mean, couldn't we bring those skills to bear on creating a more productive form of post-publication review that serves to richly and carefully describe the ongoing impact that a scholar's work is having, regardless of the venue and type of its publication? If so, some of the roadblocks to a broader acceptance of open-access publication might be broken down, or at least rendered breakdown-able.

There seem to me two key imperatives in the implementation of such a system, however, which get at the personnel-review issues that Steve is pointing to—one of them is that senior, tenured scholars have got to lead the way not just in demanding the development and acceptance of such a system, but in making use of it, in committing ourselves to publishing openly because we can; worrying about the authority or the prestige of such publishing models later. Second, we have got to present compelling arguments to our colleagues about why these models must be taken seriously—not just once, but over and over again, making sure that we've got the backs of the more junior scholars who are similarly trying to do this work.

It comes back to scholarly values. But the ethical obligation doesn't stop with publishing in open-access venues. It must extend to working to develop and establish the validity of new means of assessment appropriate to those venues.

Note

1. "ITHAKA: Faculty Survey 2009," http://www.ithaka.org/ithaka-s-r/research/faculty-surveys-2000-2009/faculty-survey-2009.

Voices

SHARING ONE'S RESEARCH

Chad Black and Mark Sample

There is a long history of scholars turning their papers over to libraries at the end of their careers. These collections are important for the two sides of historical research and publication that they represent. They provide a window into academic processes, but also access to sometimes quirky, sometimes exhaustive, primary sources, representing years of intentional collection. There is intrinsic value to such collections for both historical education and historical practice. What is more, the technologies of the web have revolutionized the potential of collections in the everyday moments of their original production. Rather than putting research processes and materials behind the veils of time, space, and limited access, we now have the possibility to construct and curate our research materials and process archives—what I call the "Papers of You," in real time, and make it immediately available to those without the resources to gain access to our eclectic collections. How would this application of technology to the small corner of disciplinary history revolutionize its part of the academy? First, making the research process transparent would open to the world the mystical reality of what it is academic historians do with their time. Additionally, making research processes and materials available would demonstrate a commitment to the scholarly values of exchange, integrity, and open access that represent the better parts of academics' nature. Distributed self-generated collections of archival material will also enhance access—particularly to resources from countries without the resources to do it all themselves. Finally, it would keep researchers honest.

—CHAD BLACK

We in the humanities are accustomed to being very secretive about our research. Sure, we go to conferences and share not-yet-published work. But these conference papers—even if they're finished the morning of the presentation with penciled-in edits—they're still addressed to an audience, meant to be shared. Are we really that ridiculous and self-important? Let's face it, I'm an English professor—it's not as if I'm working on the Manhattan Project. Imagine publishing just your research notes, shorn of context or rhetoric or (especially or) the sense of a conclusion we like to build into our papers. Imagine sharing only your works cited. Or, imagine sharing the loosest, most chaotic collection of sources, expanded far beyond the shallows of Works Cited, past the nebulous Works Consulted, deep into the fathomless Works Out There. I think that what we do—striving to understand human experience in a chaotic world—is so crucial that we need to share what we learn, every step along the way. Only then do all the lonely hours we spend tracing sources, reading, and writing make sense.

—MARK SAMPLE

Making Digital Scholarship Count

Mills Kelly

As more and more scholars do work in the digital environment they are expecting this work to count toward tenure, promotion, and other types of formal evaluation. It seems to me that the first step is to define what we actually mean when we say that digital work should "count" in higher education. At most colleges and universities around the United States—and, to varying degrees, elsewhere in the world—there are three domains of activity that faculty members engage in: research, teaching, and service. Most of us have to turn in an annual report that is organized into three sections corresponding to these domains. In varying ways at various campuses, what can be claimed in each domain is defined by the institution or by departments. Sometimes, those things that count are defined in union contracts; sometimes they are defined as they come up. In short, there is no standard practice in academia, other than to generally rely on research, teaching, and service as the main categories for faculty evaluation.

A thornier issue is how activity in each of these domains is evaluated. Here we see even more variation in practice from one campus to another; from one department to another. What counts at one place, is ignored or even penalized at another. At one institution, research trumps all; at another, teaching is the coin of the realm. In some history departments, it is enough to have published a book; in others, that book needs to be published by some relatively short list of prestigious presses. Context is everything in this discussion.

Does this mean it is hopeless to even take on the issue of how digital work might fit into such a heterogeneous set of practices? By no means.

In the history business, we have a very informal and fluid set of standards for determining what is and is not meritorious. We all know that an article published in a journal judged to be prestigious is probably more praiseworthy than one published in a backwater journal with little or no reputation. We know that a book published by a university press that has a great reputation is almost surely better than one published by a press no one has ever heard of. Or at least we think we know these things.

Whether book or article X published by a prestigious journal/press is actually better than book or article Y published by a journal/press we've not heard of is an open question. We assume in advance, though, that X is probably better than Y.

We do so not without good reason. Those things submitted for publication to a prestigious press/journal are more likely to go through a more rigorous peer-review and editorial process than something published in an underfunded and little-known press or journal. The competition to publish in the prestigious venues is keen—submissions of lesser quality get weeded out; thus it has been for generations.

As long as historians produced scholarship that was in a form that fit neatly into this model—books or journal articles published following a peer-review process—all was well, and the system functioned fairly smoothly. Then digital technology invaded the cozy confines of our discipline and things got a lot more complicated.

You may have noticed that I use the term "digital work" rather than "digital scholarship." My choice of words was in no way accidental. Digital work encompasses everything historians do in the digital realm—scholarship, teaching, and service. "Digital scholarship" is a precisely defined—or should be precisely defined—subset of "digital work."

Before we can even begin to claim that something called "digital scholarship" should count in the research domain of our professional lives, we would do well to define exactly what constitutes "scholarship." Here, I think we have an easier task. In almost any discipline, scholarship has the following characteristics: it is the result of original research; it has an argument of some sort and that argument is situated in a preexisting conversation among scholars; it is public; it is peer-reviewed; and it has an audience response.

There are exceptions, of course. A novel, a collection of poetry, a work of art, or a piece of music may all count as scholarship in certain contexts. By and large, though, the characteristics I've described hold for most forms of scholarship. This means that for digital scholarship to be scholarship it has to have all of these characteristics.

We'll return to this crucial issue later. But for now, I think it's easier to define what digital scholarship isn't than to define what it is—especially because, as we'll see, it is an inherently moving target.

I think we would all agree that a course website or a series of lectures created in one's favorite slideware program do not constitute scholarship. They may well be very scholarly, but on any campus I can think of, this sort of work falls clearly and unequivocally into the teaching domain.

Where it gets trickier is when we consider digitization projects—whether small in scale, or massive, like Tufts University's Perseus Project, or the University of Virginia's Valley of the Shadow.[1] Each of these excellent and heavily used projects offers scholars, teachers, students, and the general public unique access to their content. But, as Duke University's Cathy Davidson said in an interview, "the database is not the scholarship. The book or the article that results from it is the scholarship." Or, I would add, the digital scholarship that results from it. In other words, I'm not willing to limit us to the old warhorses of the book or scholarly article.

I also want to emphasize that I have tremendous respect for the scholars and teams of students and staff who created these two projects—both of which I use often in my own teaching. But I also have to say that I don't think either project can be considered scholarship if we use the definition I've proposed here.

Why not? you may ask. The reason is fairly simple in both cases. Neither project offers an argument. Both are amazing resources, but neither advances our understanding of particular historical questions. They make it possible for that understanding to advance in ways that weren't available before, but as Davidson says, it is what results from a project like these that is the scholarship. Thus, for instance, though the Valley of the Shadow database does not qualify as scholarship, the resulting article, "The Differences Slavery Made," published by the database's creators William Thomas and Edward Ayers in the *American Historical Review* rises to the level of scholarship in our working definition.[2]

I think that almost all historians would agree with this definition because it's the one we use all the time. We're comfortable with it, it works for us, and given how used we are to it, many historians—including many I know and respect—argue that there is no need to change it. After all, if it ain't broke, why fix it?

Alas, for our current definition of scholarship, the digital world is undermining our certainties.

The big sticking point is the next-to-the-last part of my definition—peer review. For a century or more, peer review in our discipline has meant that the historian produces his or her work—book or article—and submits it for publication. Then, after waiting months—or, more likely, many months—the historian finally receives feedback on his or her work and either has a little more work to do, a lot more work to do, or finds the work rejected entirely.

Why won't this process survive in the digital world? The answer is pretty simple. It just takes too long and does not work in a medium where gatekeeping makes no sense. By its very nature, digital scholarship happens in a dynamic space—one where the work is often self-published in the sense that a scholar or a group of scholars creates historical work in the digital environment, and then it is made available when it's done—or close enough to done to show other people. Not after a lengthy process of peer review—but when it's ready to be seen.

Then, and only then, does peer review begin. The Internet is an open environment, not the closed environment of the publishing industry that we have lived with for many generations. Anyone can publish anything online and that, of course, means that a lot of dreck appears. But the fact that dreck is scattered all over the Internet does not mean that quality work cannot also appear through the same process.

The American Historical Association is proposing to try to act as some sort of gatekeeper for digital historical scholarship, but this proposal is doomed because it is trying to find a way to fit the old system into a new technological environment where gatekeeping as we've known it doesn't—and can't—work.

Already in other industries we have seen what happens when the guardians of the old ways try to hold back the tide of change. Sales of music CDs continue to drop like a stone while sales of individual songs through services like iTunes continue to rise rapidly. A decade ago, Kodak employed four times as many workers as it does today (when was the last time you bought a roll of film?). And while Amazon hasn't killed off all local bookstores, there certainly are far fewer than there used to be.

So what, you might ask? Why do we have to change?

Because if we don't, we'll eventually become irrelevant. Already other disciplines that are not as resistant to change have embraced the digital world to a much greater extent. For example, work posted on the online Social Science Research Network "counts" in many academic departments around the country, despite the fact that peer review takes place after the fact, not before.[3] And in other disciplines—computer science, biology, physics, etc.—peer review increasingly takes other forms entirely. So why are we so hung up on keeping a system that made good sense a hundred or fifty years ago, but makes less and less sense today?

I wondered what a provost might think about this issue, so I spoke to Peter Stearns, provost at George Mason University, a past vice president of the American Historical Association (Teaching Division), the founding editor of the *Journal of Social History*, and the author of more than 100 books—so, he knows something about peer review.

He told me that being a provost meant that he had to take a much more capacious view of peer review, because each discipline at the university has its own standards for what constitutes proper peer review. What Peter cares about is not *how* the peer review happens, but that it *does happen*. "It can be either before or after publication," he said in our interview.

Other disciplines do it, so what is so particular, so unique about historical and humanities scholarship that it must be reviewed prior to publication? Upon reflection—nothing.

I'm not proposing that we throw out a system that has worked for so long in one fell swoop. I am suggesting, however, that there needs to be a serious discussion in our profession about what peer review means, what its value is to the process of advancing knowledge, and how it can change to take into account the new realities of the digital world. If we don't have this discussion—and soon—we're in danger of losing touch with a rising generation of young scholars who will see us as nothing more than cranky old scholars who are hanging onto an old system because it serves our interests—not theirs.

Notes

1. Gregory R. Crane, "Perseus Digital Library," http://www.perseus.tufts.edu/hopper/. "The Valley of the Shadow: Two Communities in the American Civil War," http://valley.lib.virginia.edu/.

2. William G. Thomas III and Edward L. Ayers, "An Overview: The Differences Slavery Made: A Close Analysis of Two American Communities," *American Historical Review* 108, no. 5. "The History Cooperative," *American Historical Review*, December 2003.

3. Social Science Research Network (SSRN), http://ssrn.com/.

Theory, Method, and Digital Humanities

Tom Scheinfeldt

The criticism most frequently leveled at digital humanities is what I like to call the "Where's the beef?" question—that is, what questions does digital humanities answer that can't be answered without it? What humanities arguments does digital humanities make?

Concern over the apparent lack of argument in digital humanities comes not only from outside our young discipline. Many practicing digital humanists are concerned about it as well. Rob Nelson of the University of Richmond's Digital Scholarship Lab, an accomplished digital humanist, ruminated in his proposal for THATCamp (The Humanities and Technology Camp) 2010, "While there have been some projects that have been developed to present arguments, they are few, and for the most part I sense that they haven't had a substantial impact among academics, at least in the field of history."[1] Another post on the *Humanist* listserv (volume 124), which has covered humanities computing for over two decades, expresses one digital humanist's "dream" of "a way of interpreting with computing that would allow arguments, real arguments, to be conducted at the micro-level and their consequences made in effect instantly visible at the macro-level."[2]

These concerns are justified. Does digital humanities have to help answer questions and make arguments? Yes, of course: that's what the humanities are all about. Is it answering lots of questions currently? Probably not: hence the reason for worry.

But this suggests another, more difficult, more nuanced question: When? When does digital humanities have to produce new arguments? Does it have to produce new arguments now? Does it have to answer questions yet?

In 1703, the great instrument maker, mathematician, and experimenter Robert Hooke died, vacating the suggestively named position he occupied for more than forty years—Curator of Experiments to the Royal Society. In this role, it was Hooke's job to prepare public demonstrations of scientific phenomena for the Fellows' meetings. Among Hooke's standbys in these scientific performances were animal dissections, demonstrations of the air pump—made famous by Robert Boyle, but made by Hooke—and viewings of preprepared microscope slides. Part research, part icebreaker, and part theater, one important function of these performances was to entertain the wealthier Fellows of the Society, many of whom were chosen for election more for their patronage than their scientific achievements.

Upon Hooke's death, the position of Curator of Experiments passed to Francis Hauksbee, who continued Hooke's program of public demonstrations. Many of Hauksbee's demonstrations involved the "electrical machine," essentially an evacuated glass globe which was turned on an axle and to which friction—a hand, a cloth, a piece of fur—was applied to produce a static electrical charge. Invented some years earlier, Hauksbee greatly improved the device to produce ever greater charges. Perhaps his most important improvement was the addition to the globe of a small amount of mercury, which produced a glow when the machine was fired up. In an age of candlelight and on a continent of long, dark winters, the creation of a new source of artificial light was sensational and became a popular learned entertainment, not only in meetings of early scientific societies, but in aristocratic parlors across Europe. Hauksbee's machine also set off an explosion of electrical instrument making, experimentation, and descriptive work in the first half of the eighteenth century by the likes of Stephen Gray, John Theophilus Desaguliers, and Pieter van Musschenbroek.

And yet, not until later in the eighteenth century and early in the nineteenth century did Franklin, Coulomb, Volta, and ultimately Faraday provide adequate theoretical and mathematical answers to the questions of electricity raised by the electrical machine and the phenomena it produced. Only after decades of tool building, experimentation, and description were the tools sufficiently articulated, and phenomena sufficiently described for theoretical arguments to be fruitfully made.

There's a moral to this story. One of the things digital humanities shares with the sciences is a heavy reliance on instruments, on tools. Sometimes new tools are built to answer preexisting questions. Sometimes, as in the case of Hauksbee's electrical machine, new questions and answers are the byproduct of the creation of new tools. Sometimes it takes a while; in which meantime tools themselves and the whiz-bang effects they produce must be the focus of scholarly attention. The eighteenth-century electrical machine was a parlor trick. Until it wasn't.

This kind of drawn out, *longue durée*, seasonal shifting between methodological and theoretical work isn't confined to the sciences. Growing up in the second half of the twentieth century, we are prone to think about our world in terms of ideologies, and our work in terms of theories. Late twentieth-century historical discourse was dominated by a succession of ideas and theoretical frameworks. This mirrored the broader cultural and political discourse in which our work was set. For most of the last seventy-five years of the twentieth century, socialism, fascism, existentialism, structuralism, poststructuralism, conservatism, and other ideologies vied with one another broadly in our politics, and narrowly at our academic conferences.

But it wasn't always so. Late nineteenth- and early twentieth-century scholarship was dominated not by big ideas, but by methodological refinement and disciplinary consolidation.

Denigrated in the later twentieth century as unworthy of serious attention by scholars, the nineteenth and early twentieth century, by contrast, took activities like philology, lexicology, and especially bibliography very seriously. Serious scholarship was concerned as much with organizing knowledge as it was with framing knowledge in a theoretical or ideological construct.

Take my subdiscipline—the history of science—as an example. Whereas the last few decades of research have been dominated by a debate over the relative merits of "constructivism"—the idea, in Jan Golinski's succinct definition in his excellent book *Making Natural Knowledge*, "that scientific knowledge is a human creation, made with available material and cultural resources, rather than simply the revelation of a natural order that is pre-given and independent of human action"—the history of science was in fact founded in an outpouring of bibliography.[3] The life work of the first great American historian of science—George Sarton—was not an idea, but a journal (*Isis*), a professional society (the History of Science Society), a department (Harvard's), a primer (his *Introduction to the History of Science*), and especially a bibliography (the *Isis Cumulative Bibliography*). Tellingly, the great work of his greatest pupil, Robert K. Merton, was an idea: the younger Merton's "Science, Technology and Society in Seventeenth Century England" defined history of technology as social history for a generation. By the time Merton was writing in the 1930s, the cultural climate had changed, and the consolidating and methodological activities of the teacher were giving way to the theoretical activities of the student.[4]

I believe we are at a similar moment of change right now—that we are entering a new phase of scholarship that will be dominated not by ideas, but once again by organizing activities, both in terms of organizing knowledge, and organizing ourselves and our work. Our difficulty in answering "where's the beef?" stems from the fact that, as digital humanities scholars, we traffic much less in new theories than in new methods. The new technology of the Internet has shifted the work of a rapidly growing number of scholars away from thinking big thoughts to forging new tools, methods, materials, techniques, and modes, or work which will enable us to harness the still unwieldy, but obviously game-changing, information technologies now sitting on our desktops and in our pockets. These concerns touch all scholars. The Roy Rosenzweig Center for History and New Media's Zotero research management tool is used by more than a million people—all of them grappling with the problem of information overload. And although much of the discussion remains informal, it's no accident that *Wikipedia* is right now one of the hottest topics for debate amongst scholars.

Perhaps most telling is the excitement that now—or really, once again—surrounds the library. The buzz among librarians these days dwarfs anything I have seen in my entire career among historians. The terms "library geek" and "sexy librarian" have gained new currency as everyone begins to recognize the potential of exciting library-centered projects like Google Books.

All of these things—collaborative encyclopedism, tool building, librarianship—fit uneasily into the standards of scholarship forged in the second half of the twentieth century. Most committees for promotion and tenure, for example, must value single authorship and the big idea more highly than collaborative work and methodological or disciplinary contribution. Even historians find it hard to internalize the fact that their own norms and values have, and will again, change over time. But change they must. In the days of George Sarton, a thorough bibliography was an achievement worthy of great respect, and an office closer to the reference desk in the library an occasion for great celebration (Sarton's small suite in Study 189 of Harvard's Widener Library was the epicenter of history of science in the United States for more than a quarter century). As we tumble deeper into the Internet age, I suspect it will be again.

Eventually, digital humanities must make arguments. It has to answer questions. But yet? Like eighteenth-century natural philosophers confronted with a deluge of strange new tools like microscopes, air pumps, and electrical machines, maybe we need time to articulate our digital apparatus, to produce new phenomena that we can neither anticipate, nor explain immediately. At the very least, we need to make room for both kinds of digital humanities—the kind that seeks to make arguments and answer questions now, and the kind that builds tools and resources with questions in mind, but only in the back of its mind, and only for later.

Notes

1. Rob Nelson, "Audiences and Arguments for Digital History," April 19, 2010, http://chnm2010.thatcamp.org/04/19/audiences-and-arguments-for-digital-history/.

2. *Humanist* listserv, volume 124, http://www.digitalhumanities.org/humanist/Archives/Current/Humanist.vol24.txt.

3. Jan Golinski, *Making Natural Knowledge: Constructivism And the History of Science* (Chicago: University of Chicago Press, 2005), 6.

4. George Sarton, *Introduction to the History of Science* (Philadelphia: Williams & Wilkins Company, 1931). Robert K. Merton, "Science, Technology and Society in Seventeenth Century England," *Osiris* 4 (January 1938): 360–632.

Hacking Teaching

Dear Students

Gideon Burton

Dear students:

I'm about to say something a college professor shouldn't say to his students, but I care about you a lot so I'm prepared to break the code and say what needs to be said: Your college experience is likely to set back your education, your career, and your creative potential. Ironically, this will be done in the name of education. You deserve to know about this! You have what it takes to reclaim, reform, and remix your education. Don't let college unplug your future!

Reality Check no. 1: The Digital World Is Your Home Campus

You already know this on some level. The campus for your education isn't made principally of buildings and books; it's made mostly of microchips and media. Any other school is a satellite now, subordinate to the main, digital campus where you reside and thrive. And since you grew up digital, you've been matriculated since the first click of a mouse button, with no need ever to graduate. Your world of learning and your world of play are seamless in the digital domain, and you are pretty much a senior on that campus, even in your teens. You spend your spare cash to get that iPhone or laptop, and you move effortlessly between virtual and physical worlds. The reality check is that physical schools and structured curricula and degree-seeking programs form a system that makes enormous demands upon you, but which is fundamentally out of sync with the fact that your identity, development, education, and success will be intimately intertwined with the digital domain.

And why shouldn't they be? No generation of youth has ever lived in a more exciting era than ours, nor learned in more compelling ways than are granted to you electronically today. Frontiers of opportunity have been opened for you through digital means that would make Cortés weep at how comparatively little spoil he carted off from the Aztecs. Each of you can reach across the planet, exploring the topography of our world with the ease of a soaring bird. You can befriend others from foreign places and cultures with the click of a key. You can get up-to-the-minute updates from a robot on Mars on your cell phone, or Google Alexandrian libraries with an ease that would surpass the fantasies of generations of scholars. You can be a spectator to the cosmos or to the local city-council meeting. But your new world does not leave you watching on the sidelines! You can share your lifestream, add your perspective to countless conversations, and have the world comment back—interacting with people who will value your ideas and your style. And what style! Modes of creative expression are being opened to your generation that none have known before. You can shape and share your identity in a thousand different ways, testing what you like, feeding your own passions, carving your own way. What a fantastic time to be alive!

Reality Check no. 2: Surviving in the Real World

Hold on. It's one thing to trick out your avatar for the metaverse of your choice or suction Limewire for some fresh tracks, but what about earning your bread? Generations of parents and high-school counselors have convinced you that college is the answer. After all, how are you going to get a job if you can't show that shiny sheepskin to the suit across the desk from you in the personnel department? Blogging won't pay the bills! Maybe not.

Reality Check no. 3: Sheepskin vs. Online Identity

It will be a long time before a college diploma is as quaint as, say, getting a public notary's stamp. But there is another system already competing with college, and it will start those bean counters in the tuition office sweating soon enough. This alternative to college credentials is as huge as the Stay Puft Marshmallow Man from *Ghostbusters*, and he's towering over the skyline right where town meets gown: online identity.

That's right. Who you are and what you've done will in the very near future be so well documented by your online activities that a resume will be redundant. The time will come when a college degree will be suspect if not complemented by an admirable online record—and I'm not talking about transcripts. Your transcripts will consist of your lifestream: your blog, your social networks, your creative work published or otherwise represented online. Cyberspace is already more real to you than the physical space of your college campus—and it is becoming so for your future employers.

Sincerely,
A concerned professor

Lectures Are Bullshit

Jeff Jarvis

The following is an excerpt from Jeff Jarvis's talk at TEDxNYED, an independent regional version of the TED conferences, with their spotlighted lectures. Jarvis took the opportunity to turn against this form of academic theater.

Right now, you're the audience and I'm lecturing. That's bullshit.

What does this remind of us of? The classroom, of course, and the entire structure of an educational system built for the industrial age, turning out students all the same, convincing them that there is one right answer—and that answer springs from the lectern. If they veer from it they're wrong; they fail.

What else does this remind us of? Media, old media: one-way, one size fits all. The public doesn't decide what's news and what's right. The journalist-as-speaker does.

We must question this very form. We must enable students to question the form. We should want questions, challenges, discussion, debate, collaboration, quests for understanding, and solutions. Has the Internet taught us any less?

But that is what education and media do: they validate. They also repeat. In news, I have argued that we can no longer afford to repeat the commodified news the public already knows because we want to tell the story under our byline, exuding our ego; we must, instead, add unique value.

The same can be said of the academic lecture. Does it still make sense for countless teachers to rewrite the same essential lecture about, say, capillary action? Used to be, they had to. But not now, not since open curricula and YouTube. Just as journalists must become more curator than creator, so must educators.

A few years ago, I had this conversation with Bob Kerrey at the New School. He asked what he could do to compete with brilliant lectures now online at MIT. I said don't complete, complement. I imagined a virtual Oxford based on a system of lecturers and tutors. Maybe the New School should curate the best lectures on capillary action from MIT and Stanford, or a brilliant teacher who explains it well even if not from a big-school brand; that could be anyone in YouTube U. Then the New School adds value by tutoring: explaining, answering, probing, enabling.

The lecture does have its place to impart knowledge and get us to a shared starting point. But it's not the be all and end all of education—or journalism. Now the shared lecture is a way to find efficiency in ending repetition, to make the best use of the precious teaching resources we have, to highlight and support the best. I'll give the same advice to the academy that I give to news media: Do what you do best and link to the rest.

I still haven't moved past the lecture and teacher as starting point. I also think we must make the students the starting point.

At a Carnegie event at the Paley Center a few weeks ago, I moderated a panel on teaching entrepreneurial journalism and it was only at the end of the session that I realized what I should have done: start with the room, not the stage. I asked the students in the room what they wished their schools were teaching them. It was a great list: practical, yet visionary.

So we need to move students up the education chain. They don't always know what they need to know, but why don't we start by finding out? Instead of giving tests to find out what they've learned, we should test to find out what they don't know. Their wrong answers aren't failures—they are needs and opportunities.

But the problem is that we start at the end, at what we think students should learn, prescribing and preordaining the outcome: we have the list of right answers. We tell them our answers before they've asked the questions. We drill them and test them and tell them they've failed if they don't regurgitate back our lectures as lessons learned. That is a system built for the industrial age, for the assembly line, stamping out everything the same: students as widgets, all the same.

But we are no longer in the industrial age. We are in the Google age. Hear Jonathan Rosenberg, Google's head of product management, who advised students in a blog post. Google, he said, is looking for "non-routine problem-solving skills." The routine way to solve the problem of misspelling is, of course, the dictionary. The nonroutine way is to listen to all the mistakes and corrections we make and feed that back to us in the miraculous, "Did you mean?"

"In the real world," he said, "the tests are all open book, and your success is inexorably determined by the lessons you glean from the free market." "It's easy to educate for the routine, and hard to educate for the novel," Rosenberg adds. Google sprung from seeing the novel. Is our educational system preparing students to work for or create Googles? Googles don't come from lectures.

So if not the lecture hall, what's the model? I mentioned one—the distributed Oxford—lectures here, teaching there.

Once you're distributed, then one has to ask, why have a university? Why have a school? Why have a newspaper? Why have a place or a thing? Perhaps, like a new news organization, the tasks shift from creating and controlling content and managing scarcity to curating people and content, and enabling an abundance of students, teachers, and knowledge: a world where anyone can teach and everyone will learn. We must stop selling scarce chairs in lecture halls and thinking that is our value.

We must stop our culture of standardized testing and standardized teaching. Fuck the SATs. In the Google age, what is the point of teaching memorization?

We must stop looking at education as a product—in which we turn out every student giving the same answer—to a process, in which every student looks for new answers. Life is a perpetual beta.

Why shouldn't every university—every school—copy Google's 20 percent rule, encouraging and enabling creation and experimentation, with every student expected to make a book, or an opera, or an algorithm, or a company? Rather than showing our diplomas, shouldn't we show our portfolios of work as a far better expression of our thinking and capability? The school becomes not a factory, but an incubator.

From Knowledgeable to Knowledge-able

Michael Wesch

Most university classrooms have gone through a massive transformation in the past ten years. I'm not talking about the numerous initiatives for multiple plasma screens, moveable chairs, round tables, or digital whiteboards. The change is visually more subtle, yet potentially much more transformative. I recently wrote about this in an *Encyclopædia Britannica* online forum.

> There is something in the air, and it is nothing less than the digital artifacts of over one billion people and computers networked together collectively producing over 2,000 gigabytes of new information per second. While most of our classrooms were built under the assumption that information is scarce and hard to find, nearly the entire body of human knowledge now flows through and around these rooms in one form or another, ready to be accessed by laptops, cellphones, and iPods. Classrooms built to re-enforce the top-down authoritative knowledge of the teacher are now enveloped by a cloud of ubiquitous digital information where knowledge is made, not found, and authority is continuously negotiated through discussion and participation.[1]

This new media environment can be enormously disruptive to our current teaching methods and philosophies. As we increasingly move toward an environment of instant and infinite information, it becomes less important for students to know, memorize, or recall information, and more important for them to be able to find, sort, analyze, share, discuss, critique, and create information. They need to move from being simply knowledgeable to being knowledge-*able*.

The sheer quantity of information now permeating our environment is astounding, but more importantly, networked digital information is also qualitatively different than information in other forms. It has the potential to be created, managed, read, critiqued, and organized very differently than information on paper, and to take forms that we have not yet even imagined. To understand the true potentials of this information revolution on higher education, we need to look beyond the framework of "information." For at the base of this information revolution are new ways of relating to one another; new forms of discourse; new ways of interacting; new kinds of groups; and new ways of sharing, trading, and collaborating. Wikis, blogs, tagging, social networking, and other developments that fall under the Web 2.0 buzz are especially promising in this regard because they are inspired by a spirit of interactivity, participation, and collaboration. It is this spirit of Web 2.0 which is important to education. The technology is secondary.

This is a social revolution, not a technological one, and its most revolutionary aspect may be the ways in which it empowers us to rethink education and the teacher-student relationship in an almost limitless variety of ways.

Physical, Social, and Cognitive Structures Working Against Us

Yet there are many structures working against us. Our physical structures were built prior to an age of infinite information, our social structures formed to serve different purposes than those needed now, and the cognitive structures we have developed along the way now struggle to grapple with the emerging possibilities.

The physical structures are easiest to see, and are on prominent display in any large "state-of-the-art" classroom. Rows of fixed chairs often face a stage or podium housing a computer from which the professor controls at least 786,432 points of light on a massive screen. Stadium seating, sound-absorbing panels, and other acoustic technologies are designed to draw maximum attention to the professor at the front of the room. The message of this environment is that to learn is to acquire information, that information is scarce and hard to find (that's why you have to come to this room to get it), that you should trust authority for good information, and that good information is beyond discussion (that's why the chairs don't move or turn toward one another). In short, it tells students to trust authority and follow along.

This is a message that very few faculty could agree with, and in fact some may use the room to launch spirited attacks against it. But the content of such talks is overshadowed by the ongoing hour-to-hour and day-to-day practice of sitting and listening to an authority for information, then regurgitating that information on exams.

Many faculty may hope to subvert the system, but a variety of social structures work against them. Radical experiments in teaching carry no guarantees, and even fewer rewards in most tenure and promotion systems, even if they are successful. In many cases, faculty are required to assess their students in a standardized way to fulfill requirements for the curriculum. Nothing is easier to assess than information recall on multiple-choice exams, and the concise and "objective" numbers satisfy committee members busy with their own teaching and research.

Even in situations in which a spirit of exploration and freedom exist, where faculty are free to experiment to work beyond physical and social constraints, our cognitive habits often get in the way. Marshall McLuhan called it "the rear-view mirror effect," noting that "We see the world through a rear-view mirror. We march backwards into the future."[2]

Most of our assumptions about information are based on characteristics of information on paper. On paper, we thought of information as a "thing" with a material form, and we created elaborate hierarchies to classify each piece of information in its own logical place. But as David Weinberger—in his book *Everything Is Miscellaneous*, and Clay Shirky—in his essay "Ontology Is Overrated," have demonstrated, networked digital information is fundamentally different than information on paper.[3] And each digital innovation seems to shake us free from yet another assumption we once took for granted.

Even something as simple as the hyperlink taught us that information can be in more than one place at one time, challenging our traditional space-time-based notions of information as a "thing" that has to be "in a place." Google began harnessing the links and revolutionized our research with powerful machine-assisted searching.

Blogging came along and taught us that anybody can be a creator of information. Suddenly anybody can create a blog in a matter of seconds—and people have responded. Technorati now reports that there are over 133 million blogs—almost 133 million more than there were just five years ago. YouTube and other video-sharing sites have sparked similar widespread participation in the production of video. Over 10,000 hours of video are uploaded to the web every day. In the past six months, more material has been uploaded to YouTube than all of the content ever aired on major network television. While such media beg for participation, our lecture halls are still sending the message, "follow along."

Wikipedia has taught us yet another lesson: that a networked information environment allows people to work together in new ways to create information that can rival—and even surpass—the content of experts by almost any measure. The message of *Wikipedia* is not "trust authority," but "explore authority." Authorized information is not beyond discussion on *Wikipedia*, information is authorized through discussion, and this discussion is available for the world to see and even participate in. This culture of discussion and participation is now available on any website with the emerging "second layer" of the web through applications like Diigo, which allow you to add notes and tags to any website, anywhere.

As we note and tag these sites, we are also collectively organizing them, so that the notion that this new media environment is too big and disorganized for anybody to find anything worthwhile and relevant is simply not the case. Our old assumption that information is hard to find is trumped by the realization that if we set up our hyperpersonalized digital network effectively, *information can find us*. For example, I have set up my own Netvibes portal so that the moment anybody anywhere tags something with certain keywords I am interested in I will immediately receive a link to the item. It is like continuously working with thousands of research associates around the world.

Taken together, this new media environment demonstrates to us that the idea of learning as acquiring information is no longer a message we can afford to send to our students, and that we need to start redesigning our learning environments to address, leverage, and harness the new media environment now permeating our classrooms.

A Crisis of Significance

Unfortunately, many teachers only see the disruptive possibilities of these technologies when they find students Facebooking, texting, IMing, or shopping during class. Though many blame the technology, these activities are just new ways for students to tune out—part of the much bigger problem I have called "the crisis of significance"—the fact that many students are now struggling to find meaning and significance in their education. Nothing good will come of these technologies if we do not first confront the crisis of significance and bring relevance back into education. In some ways, these technologies act as magnifiers. If we fail to address the crisis of significance, the technologies will only magnify the problem by allowing students to tune out more easily and completely. With total and constant access to their entire network of friends, we might as well be walking into the food court in the student union and trying to hold their attention. On the other hand, if we work with students to find and address problems that are real and significant to them, they can then leverage the networked information environment in ways that will help them achieve the "knowledge-ability" we hope for them.

We have had our why's, how's, and what's upside-down, focusing too much on what should be learned, then how, and often forgetting the why altogether. In a world of nearly infinite information, we must first address why, facilitate how, and let the what generate naturally from there. As infinite information shifts us away from a narrow focus on information, we begin to recognize the importance of the *form* of learning over the *content* of learning. It isn't that content is not important; it is simply that it must not take precedence over form. But even as we shift our focus to the "how" of learning, there is still the question of "what" is to be learned. After all, our courses have to be *about* something. Usually our courses are arranged around subjects. In *Teaching as a Subversive Activity*, Neil Postman and Charles Weingartner note that the notion of subjects has the unwelcome effect of teaching our students that "English is not History and History is not Science and Science is not Art . . . and a subject is something you 'take' and, when you have taken it, you have 'had' it." Always aware of the hidden metaphors underlying our most basic assumptions, they suggest calling this "the Vaccination Theory of Education," as students are led to believe that once they have "had" a subject they are immune to it and need not take it again.[4]

Not Subjects but Subjectivities

As an alternative, I like to think that we are not teaching subjects but subjectivities: ways of approaching, understanding, and interacting with the world. Subjectivities cannot be taught. They involve an introspective intellectual throw down in the minds of students. Learning a new subjectivity is often painful because it almost always involves what psychologist Thomas Szasz referred to in *The Second Sin* as "an injury to one's self-esteem."[5]

To illustrate what I mean by subjectivities over subjects, I have created a list of subjectivities that I am trying to help students attain while learning the "subject" of anthropology: (1) Our worldview is not natural and unquestionable, but culturally and historically specific. (2) We are globally interconnected in ways we often do not realize. (3) Different aspects of our lives and culture are connected and affect one another deeply. (4) Our knowledge is always incomplete and open to revision. We are the creators of our world. (5) Participation in the world is not a choice, only how we participate is our choice.

Even a quick scan of these subjectivities will reveal that they can only be learned, explored, and adopted through practice. We can't teach them. We can only create environments in which the practices and perspectives are nourished, encouraged, or inspired (and therefore continually practiced).

My own experiments in this regard led to the creation of the World Simulation, now the centerpiece of my Introduction to Cultural Anthropology course at Kansas State University. As the name implies, the world simulation is an activity in which we try to simulate the world. Of course, in order to simulate the world, we need to know everything we can about it. So while the course is set up much like a typical cultural anthropology course, moving through the same readings and topics, all of these learnings are ultimately focused around one big question, "How does the world work?"

Students are cocreators of every aspect of the simulation, and are asked to harness and leverage the new media environment to find information, theories, and tools we can use to answer our big question. Each student has a specific role and expertise to develop. A world map is superimposed on the class, and each student is asked to become an expert on a specific aspect of the region in which they find themselves. Using this knowledge, they work in 15 to 20 small groups to create realistic cultures, step-by-step, as we go through each aspect of culture in class. This allows them to apply the knowledge they learn in the course and to recognize the ways different aspects of culture—economic, social, political, and religious practices and institutions—are integrated in a cultural system.

In the final weeks of the course, we explore how different cultures around the world are interconnected and how they relate to one another. Students continue to harness and leverage the new media environment to learn more about these interconnections, and use the wiki to work together to create the "rules" for our simulation. They face the daunting task of creating a way to simulate colonization, revolution, the emergence of a global economy, war and diplomacy, and environmental challenges. Along the way, they are exploring some of the most important challenges now facing humanity.

The World Simulation itself only takes 75–100 minutes, and moves through 650 metaphorical years—1450–2100. It is recorded by students on twenty digital video cameras and edited into one final "world history" video using clips from real-world history to illustrate the correspondences. We watch the video together in the final weeks of the class, using it as a discussion starter for contemplating our world and our role in its future. By then it seems as if we have the whole world right before our eyes in one single classroom—profound cultural differences, profound economic differences, profound challenges for the future, and one humanity. We find ourselves not just as cocreators of a simulation, but as cocreators of the world itself, and the future is up to us.

Managing a learning environment such as this poses its own unique challenges, but there is one simple technique, which makes everything else fall into place: *love and respect your students and they will love and respect you back.* With the underlying feeling of trust and respect this provides, students quickly realize the importance of their role as cocreators of the learning environment, and they begin to take responsibility for their own education.

New Models of Assessment for New Media Environments: The Next Frontier

All of this vexes traditional criteria for assessment and grades. This is the next frontier as we try to transform our learning environments. When I speak frankly with professors all over the world, I find that, like me, they often find themselves jury-rigging old assessment tools to serve the new needs brought into focus by a world of infinite information. Content is no longer king, but many of our tools have been habitually used to measure content recall. For example, I have often found myself writing content-based multiple-choice questions in a way that I hope will indicate that the student has mastered a new subjectivity or perspective. Of course, the results are not satisfactory. More importantly, these questions ask students to waste great amounts of mental energy memorizing content instead of exercising a new perspective in the pursuit of real and relevant questions.

Of course, multiple-choice questions are an easy target for criticism, but even more sophisticated measures of cognitive development may miss the point. When you watch somebody who is truly "in it" —somebody who has totally given themselves over to the learning process—or if you simply imagine those moments in which you were "in it" yourself, you immediately recognize that learning expands far beyond the mere cognitive dimension. These additional dimensions, as Randy Bass noted in his introduction to the January 2009 issue of *Academic Commons*, include "emotional and affective dimensions, capacities for risk-taking and uncertainty, creativity and invention," and more.[6] How will we assess these? I do not have the answers, but a renewed and spirited dedication to the creation of authentic learning environments that leverage the new media environment demands that we address it.

The new media environment provides new opportunities for us to create a community of learners with our students seeking important and meaningful questions. Questions of the very best kind abound, and we become students again, pursuing questions we might have never imagined, joyfully learning right along with the others. In the best case scenario the students will leave the course, not with answers, but with more questions, and even more importantly, the capacity to ask still more questions generated from their continual pursuit and practice of the subjectivities we hope to inspire. This is what I have called elsewhere "anti-teaching," in which the focus is not on providing answers to be memorized, but on creating a learning environment more conducive to producing the types of questions that ask students to challenge their taken-for-granted assumptions and see their own underlying biases.

The beauty of the current moment is that new media has thrown all of us as educators into just this kind of question-asking, bias-busting, assumption-exposing environment. There are no easy answers, but we can at least be thankful for the questions that drive us on.

Notes

1. *Encyclopædia Britannica Blog*, "A Vision of Students Today (& What Teachers Must Do)," blog entry by Michael Wesch, October 21, 2008, http://www.britannica.com/blogs/2008/10/a-vision-of-students-today-what-teachers-must-do/.

2. Marshall McLuhan and Quentin Fiore, *The Medium Is the Massage* (New York: Bantam, 1967).

3. Clay Shirky, "Ontology Is Overrated—Categories, Links, and Tags," http://www.shirky.com/writings/ontology_overrated.html. David Weinberger, *Everything Is Miscellaneous: The Power of the New Digital Disorder,* 1st ed. (New York: Times Books, 2007).

4. Neil Postman and Charles Weingartner, *Teaching as a Subversive Activity* (New York: Delacorte Press, 1969), 21.

5. Thomas Stephen Szasz, *The Second Sin* (New York and London: Routledge, 1974), 18.

6. Randy Bass, "New Media Technologies and the Scholarship of Teaching and Learning: A Brief Introduction to This Issue of Academic Commons," *Academic Commons,* January 7, 2009, http://www.academiccommons.org/commons/essay/introduction-issue.

Voices

CLASSROOM ENGAGEMENT

Mills Kelly, David Doria, Rey Junco

Sometimes it seems to me that whenever things go wrong in college teaching, the first impulse of the professor is to blame the students. They aren't prepared for class. They don't want to grapple with the hard concepts. They don't want to read what I assign. They do all their work at the last minute. And now come laptops, smartphones, and other digital devices. We've all seen it. The student with a laptop who has clearly checked out of lecture. Is he reading his email? Is she chatting with a friend? Is he playing *World of Warcraft*? And then there are the other students peering covertly or openly at the open screen. I'm sorry to report that laptops aren't the problem, nor are students. Instead of blaming our students for wandering away on their laptops, it's time we looked a little more closely in the mirror and asked ourselves *why* they wander off. Let's take a step back and stop blaming our students—and their laptops. Doing so will force us to think more carefully about our own teaching practice and how we—as opposed to they—might improve.

—MILLS KELLY

It has always seemed extremely odd and unacceptable to many of us that faculty members of most universities, while being experts in their areas of research, have not received even a single hour of training on how to be an effective educator. In any other occupation, training is an intensely integral part of the job. Airplane pilots must log thousands and thousands of hours in simulators and in simple planes before they are allowed to fly commercial jets. There are even federal regulations to ensure that every airplane pilot is not only trained appropriately, but also can demonstrate that his training has resulted in him being an excellent pilot. However, for arguably the most important job—educating the next generation—no one blinks an eye at the zero hours of training logged by the pilots of the classrooms.

—DAVID DORIA

Faculty need to be more like hackers. The old-school conceptualization of the classroom as a place to receive knowledge has outlived its usefulness. Society in general, and today's college students specifically, are more interested in participatory methodologies. Students are able to participate in their consumption of information from other sources, why not allow—better yet, encourage—them to participate in the consumption of academic information? Furthermore, most of today's college students have never known a time without the communications technologies that are blended into their lifestyles. There is evidence that high media users and multitaskers have different information-processing styles than low users. Ask any pilot and they will tell you that it is surprising how well humans can adapt to situations where we need to divide our attention between various tasks. There's an old pilot saying that "driving a car is like sleeping compared to flying." Now, imagine your students processing information like pilots. In a typical day they are connecting, consuming, and creating in the digital space paying attention to many things at once. Then, they walk into the college classroom where things move a lot slower and engagement demands are low (possibly near zero). Can we blame them for being disengaged?

—REY JUNCO

Digital Literacy and the Undergraduate Curriculum

Jeff McClurken, Jeremy Boggs, Adrianne Wadewitz, Anne Ellen Geller, Jon Beasley-Murray

Digital Literacy and the Undergraduate Curriculum

—Jeff McClurken

The notion of digital literacy is sometimes criticized for being overused and having multiple definitions. Those are real problems, but they are also opportunities. I actually like the phrase for people's familiarity with it and for that very richness of meanings, and I've viewed the goals of my undergraduate digital history course through some of those definitions.

One goal of my digital history course is to teach the most conventional form of digital literacy: How does one find and evaluate online materials for scholarly—and nonscholarly—uses? How does one begin to sift through the massive content that is available in a systematic and/or creative way? What are the pitfalls and perils, the promises and potentialities of the online information experience?

Another facet of digital literacy is the notion of digital identity: This is a class that, through individual and group online presence—often blogs and wikis, but many other tools are available as well—explicitly engages students in discussions of their digital identity. How should we present ourselves to the online world—personally, professionally, and intellectually, but also individually, and in groups? In future iterations, it might encourage them to create their own centralized online presence that wouldn't necessarily be housed by the university—or restricted by a single course. We've been engaged recently at University of Mary Washington in a number of discussions related to this notion of enabling students to take control of their digital identity.

Increasingly, I have become convinced that a key, but often overlooked, aspect of digital literacy is a willingness to experiment with a variety of online tools, and then to think critically and strategically about a project, and to identify those tools that would be most useful to that project. Note that I'm not talking about training in a specific tool or even a set of tools. This is not a Microsoft Word or Blackboard skills class. This digital history class offers students a "digital toolkit" from which to choose. There certainly needs to be some basic exposure and technical support, but part of the goal is to get students to figure out how a new tool—system, software, historical process—works on their own.

Broadening the previous point, one of my desires for students is for them to be comfortable with being uncomfortable as they try new things. Figuring how to deal with constantly changing technology is something we all are dealing with, yet in higher education we often put students in new situations only when they first begin. Before long, they've got the process and procedures down, and can churn out eight- to ten-page papers in their sleep. Yet what kind of preparation is that for the larger world? I know, I know. There are much larger philosophical and practical and even political issues at work here. But my point is simply that it's good for college classes to shake students—and faculty—out of their comfort zone. Real learning happens when you're trying to figure out the controls, not when you're on autopilot.

Finally, I think digital literacy for undergraduates in history should encompass at least some exposure to the complex new approaches to research in the discipline offered by recent advancements in computing, including text mining or GIS—if only because those methods are influencing a new generation of scholarship that students will need to understand. As they become more accessible and widely used, there will be more opportunities for students to also engage in the application of these tools in their own work.

Three Roles for Teachers Using Technology

—Jeremy Boggs

Instructor as Role Model

I think any instructor using technology, in the class or out, should think of themselves as a role model for how those technologies can be used for responsible, beneficial goals. One way I do this is to be completely transparent with students regarding my use of technology. I provide links to my blog, Twitter account, Flickr account, YouTube and Vimeo usernames, Facebook page, and my instant-messenger screennames. I encourage them to follow me, and contact me through any of these methods. I set up rules for contacting me, though, which are followed 99.9 percent of the time, and that 0.1 percent is not enough of a problem for me to change my transparency. I also show students how I've used my blog, Twitter feed, and other accounts to build a professional network and share information. While others warn about the ill effects of putting too much of yourself online—which can be true—I try to show students how I use technology to expand my opportunities, not limit them. Overall, I've had positive feedback from students about my openness. I think that I use technology and social media responsibly—though I could work on the efficiency part. Setting an example that students can follow is important if we want those students to be more critical about their use of technology.

Instructor as Tech Support

When utilizing social media and technology in my courses, I've found myself serving as the primary tech-support person when students run into trouble. With my tech background, I'm comfortable with this, but I suspect a lot of teachers are not. Explaining the technical aspects of blogging, wikis, RSS feeds, YouTube, and Flickr can take up time spent on other things in class and out, but I think it's very important to take on this role. In a lot of cases, support involves me showing students how to find answers to their questions on the web, on support forums, or other resources. In other cases, support involves me taking five–ten minutes at the end of class to explain how a particular technology works. While this can be an enormous amount of work, serving as tech support has, I think, given my students more confidence in my ability to teach with and use technology (going back to Instructor as Role Model).

For example, I have an assignment that asks students to research and write an article on *Wikipedia*. It's not a big article—around 500 words—but the assignment does ask a lot from students such as: learn how to do proper formatting for *Wikipedia*, research an article, and try as hard as they can to ensure their article isn't vandalized or deleted, and encourage other users to contribute to the article. Learning these things requires a lot of my time for tech support: explain how *Wikipedia* works; how to format footnotes, headings, et cetera; and how to find guidelines to follow if a student's article is up for deletion. This is not the kind of task I'd ask of university tech support, because the assignment is as much about learning these technical things as it is learning about collaborative writing and research. The fact that I can take on a role of tech support helps make the assignment successful.

Instructor as Cheerleader

Out of the three, I think the role of Instructor as Cheerleader is the most important. I really think that there's a lack of cheerleading or positive reinforcement in higher education in general, particularly when trying to teach students to use new kinds of technology or social media. At the beginning of the semester, usually after the first class when I've introduced all the things we'll be doing with computers, I get a few emails from students saying something to the effect that "I'm not good with all this computer stuff." And they probably aren't; I'm not convinced that this generation, like previous generations, is that tech savvy. But I do think every student I have is capable of becoming more proficient with technology than before they entered my class, and can learn how to use the technology they're exposed to every day in new, meaningful, efficient ways.

The prospect of editing a *Wikipedia* article, to return to that example, is a strange—and sometimes frightening—proposition for my students. Learning how to format footnotes in *Wikipedia*, insert images, and write the proper code for headings and bulleted lists can be daunting to many, let alone connecting with a few dozen completely unknown Wikipedians to discuss the merits of their articles as some face deletion. Encouragement and genuine interest in the success of each student's project is imperative, as is patience. There may be some hand-holding involved as students negotiate with sometime rude *Wikipedia* admins—I've done this—or spending some extra time during office hours explaining wiki formatting while encouraging students that they are in fact smart enough to do all this computer stuff—I've also done this. Pointing out successes in class, even if it's as simple as successfully inserting a YouTube clip into a blog post, goes a long way to get students vested in the assignments, and class as a whole.

Results

All of these roles help me accomplish one of my goals in class: help my students become more savvy, more responsible consumers and producers of media and technology. I think trading of some time covering some particular historical topic to teach students how to extend learning beyond my classroom is more than worth it. In the end, I get more students interested in exploring history, and help shape more responsible social-technology users. Even if I only influence a handful of students, I'll consider my class a success.

Opening Up the Academy with *Wikipedia*

—Adrianne Wadewitz, Anne Ellen Geller, Jon Beasley-Murray

Like an uninvited guest at a party, *Wikipedia* hovers at the fringes of academia. Yet the online encyclopedia's aims are eminently academic: it collects, processes, stores, and transmits knowledge. Judging by the site's three-million-plus articles, many of which are extensively referenced to the scholarly literature, and its popularity on the Internet, *Wikipedia* has been remarkably successful at promoting a culture that honors intellectual inquiry, yet it is derided by many academics.

Still, we all use *Wikipedia* in one way or another—even scholars, although we might not want to admit to the fact. Most of us find it a very convenient resource. Above all, students use *Wikipedia*, openly or otherwise; as Alison J. Head and Michael B. Eisenberg wrote for *First Monday* in 2010, over half of U.S. undergraduates use it "always" or "frequently" in their research.[1] However, these students do so without necessarily knowing how the information is written and revised. They are often told not to use *Wikipedia* because it is "bad"—but they are not told why.

We do not want to debate whether or not *Wikipedia* is a reliable source for research: we agree that it is not. However, many academics use *Wikipedia* as a *first* source on a topic with which they are unfamiliar. The extent to which *Wikipedia* is a credible source is one of many conversations about *Wikipedia* we can enter into with our students—but it is not the most interesting. Such discussions are already a *de rigueur* part of any research assignment, since we raise the same questions regarding other online sources such as blogs and other self-published websites. The deeper, more interesting conversations we want to foster with our students are about how, and by whom, knowledge is created and gatekept.

We three have welcomed *Wikipedia* into our teaching in structured ways, as have other teachers and academics referenced in this volume. What we all share is the belief that incorporating *Wikipedia* into our teaching is a form of hacking the academy, giving those who contribute to *Wikipedia*—Wikipedians—a mechanism by which to bypass the typical, hierarchical routes of knowledge construction and to become knowledge makers themselves.

Students who analyze *Wikipedia* articles and participate in their development are made aware of the construction of knowledge and the ends towards which it is put. Most students utilize *Wikipedia* only to find information, and therefore have little understanding of how the articles are developed, who develops them, or the oftentimes extensive discussion and review that goes into making an article. For example, many students are unaware that every article on *Wikipedia* has an associated "discussion" page, also known as a "talk" page. Such pages are filled with ongoing conversations about the development and revision of the articles; introducing students to them is an excellent way to begin a conversation about what knowledge is, and who makes it. For example, asking students to analyze the threads on discussion pages shows them that there are often multiple narratives about a particular historical event or person, and that these competing narratives have important political valences.

As with any research paper, students learned the basics of researching, citing, summarizing, and quoting. However, because they were doing this on *Wikipedia*, unique learning experiences were offered. The premise of the project was that students had been using *Wikipedia* as a source without properly considering its drawbacks. So it should come as no surprise that, when seeking sources for the *Wikipedia* articles they were writing, students all too often made analogous mistakes of scholarship. They added information that was unsourced, poorly referenced, or even plagiarized, or they resorted to referencing other web pages and online encyclopedias.

Yet herein lay a great benefit of the assignment. Because *Wikipedia* asks that assertions be referenced, students were forced to reveal their sources. These poor sources might never have been revealed, had the students been writing a term paper. Moreover, because writing on *Wikipedia* is a process of continual revision, they could be asked to go back and reevaluate their sources, find better ones, and try again. Even with plagiarism, there was no longer a need to make a fuss, because at no time were they handing in what purported to be a final product. They simply had to start over.

In short, the assignment not only reveals the weaknesses in students' research skills, but also teaches them those skills. It shows them that research—like writing—is a process, often a lengthy one. Although you might start with suboptimal—such as *Wikipedia* itself—you progress to look for ever stronger evidence for the information at hand, or for new information that the first sources did not reveal.

Note

1. Alison J. Head and Michael B. Eisenberg, "How Today's College Students Use Wikipedia for Course-related Research," *First Monday* 15, no. 3 (March 2010), http://firstmonday.org/htbin/cgiwrap/bin/ojs/index.php/fm/article/view/2830/2476.

What's Wrong with Writing Essays

A CONVERSATION

Mark Sample and Kelly Schrum

What's Wrong with Writing
—Mark Sample

I have become increasingly disillusioned with the traditional student paper. Just as the only thing a standardized test measures is how well you can take a standardized test, the only thing a student essay measures is how well a student can conform to the rigid thesis/defense model that—surprise!—eliminates complexity, ambiguity, and most traces of critical thinking.

I don't believe that my mission as a professor is to turn my students into miniature versions of myself or of any other professor, yet that is the only function that the traditional student essay serves. And even if I did want to churn out little professors, the essay fails exceedingly well at this. Somehow the student essay has come to stand in for all the research, dialogue, revision, and work that professional scholars engage in. It doesn't.

The student essay is a twitch in a void. A compressed outpouring of energy—if we're lucky—that means nothing to no one. My friend and occasional collaborator Randy Bass has said that nowhere but school would we ask somebody to write something that nobody will ever read.

This is the primary reason I've integrated more and more public writing into my classes. I strive to instill in my students the sense that what they think and what they say and what they write matters—to me, to them, to their classmates, and through open-access blogs and wikis—to the world.

In addition to making student writing public, I've also begun taking the words out of writing. Why must writing, especially writing that captures critical thinking, be composed of words? Why not images? Why not sound? Why not objects? The word *text*, after all, derives from the Latin

"Captain's log." Photograph courtesy of Mark Sample.

textus, meaning that which is woven, strands of different material intertwined together. Let the warp be words and the weft be something else entirely.

With this in mind, I am moving away from asking students to write toward asking them to *weave*. To build, to fabricate, to design. I don't want my students to become miniature scholars. I want them to be aspiring Rauschenbergs, assembling mixed-media combines, all the while through their engagement with seemingly incongruous materials developing a critical thinking practice about the process and the product.

For instance, I asked students to design an abstract visualization of an NES video game, a kind of model that would capture some of the game's complexity and reveal underlying patterns to the way actions, space, and time unfold in the game. One student "mapped" *Sid Meier's Pirates!* onto a piece of driftwood. This "captain's log," covered with screenshots and overlaid with axes measuring time and action, evokes the static nature of the game more than words ever can. Like Meier's *Civilization*, much of *Pirates!* is given over to configurations, selecting from menus, and other nondiegetic actions. Pitched battles on the high seas—what would seem to be the highlight of any game about pirates—are rare, and though a flat photograph of the log doesn't do justice to the actual object in all its physicality, you can see some of that absence of action here, where the top of the log is full of blank wood.

What's Right with Digital Storytelling
—Kelly Schrum

As Mark Sample eloquently points out, student essays generally measure how well students conform to a standard model of essay writing far more than they measure students' ability to think critically, explore complexity and ambiguity, and engage as learners.

One of my goals in teaching a graduate-level digital storytelling (DST) class at George Mason University was to experiment with digital storytelling as a substantive, content-rich assignment.

A short project early in the semester asked students to tell a story in five photos—along the lines of the Flickr group "Tell a Story with 5 Photos for Educators."[1] One student told a tale of two goldfish bowls entitled *An Escape*.

©shutterstock/khz.

©shutterstock/newphotoservice

©shutterstock/newphotoservice

©shutterstock/newphotoservice

©shutterstock/Sergej Khakimullin

The fish leaves a crowded fishbowl to explore a solitary life. After swimming alone, though, the fish returns to group, choosing companionship over solitude.

But this is what happens when the pictures are rearranged.

©shutterstock/newphotoservice

©shutterstock/newphotoservice

©shutterstock/Sergej Khakimullin

Leader goldfish. ©shutterstock/khz

©shutterstock/newphotoservice

The images tell a very different story.

We experimented with this in class, arranging and rearranging several sets of photos. For some of the nineteen master's and doctoral students from the Department of History and Art History and the Higher Education Program, this was their first experience telling a story visually. As simple as it was, it started the process of shifting their thinking from a text-based world to one in which images tell stories and communicate meaning. This was one step of many on the path to creating the final project, a ten-minute digital story.

For me, one of the successes in the class was seeing the projects grow and develop, watching students grapple with and learn to utilize the digital medium. As students developed project pitches, scripts, and storyboards and then moved into production to create rough cuts and final projects, they experimented with a process that changed their thinking about their topics, as well as about the nature of producing knowledge. The process was intentionally scaffolded to emphasize experimentation, reflection, peer feedback, and iterative learning. At each stage, students examined their purpose, intended audience, main point, and narrative arc, and received instructor and peer feedback, pushing them to create stronger projects; more compelling pieces that engaged the digital in the storytelling.

One student, for example, chose to explore competing scholarly interpretations of *Primavera*, painted by Italian Renaissance artist Sandro Botticelli in the late fifteenth century.

The initial script read like an academic article: introducing, comparing, and contrasting academic analyses of the painting with long scholarly quotes. Through conversations, feedback, and the experience of watching a host of digital stories—the good, the bad, and the ugly—the student reexamined her approach and began to investigate strategies for maximizing the potential of DST to tell this story.

This process also surfaced the student's larger goals: to make art history accessible, and to empower viewers without a background in art history to ask questions about the broader context of paintings and their meaning.

The process of creating a digital story forced the student to confront these questions, and in the end, she created a lively digital tale that put the painting into a simulated courtroom trial as Exhibit A. Art historians served as "witnesses," explaining how and why they interpreted the painting in specific ways, presenting their credentials and the evidence for their arguments. Visually and through "testimony," the story explored debates over the painting, such as whether the third figure from the right represented the personification of spring or the goddess Flora, and whether the figure on the far left represented Hermes or Mercury. The "jury" (viewer) was asked to evaluate the testimony and competing narratives, but also to consider the constructed nature of meaning and the process of scholarly discourse.

Sandro Botticelli, *Primavera*, 1477. Used with permission by Art Resource, New York.

DST challenged students to think in new ways, to ask new questions, and to interrogate the sources and ideas they were reading, researching, and developing. It challenged students to use their academic interests and research to tell a compelling story digitally—one that both made a clear argument, and fully utilized the tools and power of digital storytelling.

One story by Rwany Sibaja explored the protest movement started by mothers and grandmothers of the 30,000 *desaparecidos*—those who disappeared during the military dictatorship of Jorge Rafael Videla. Integrating video of the protests, interviews with former military officials defending their actions, and footage of the 1978 World Cup in Argentina, the story presents a powerful historical narrative, contrasting a nation's celebration with ongoing persecution, and exploring the complicated nature of history when examined through multiple lenses.[2]

Another, "Re-inventing the Lecture (Or, Why Online Lectures Don't Work, and What We Can Do About It)," by Tad Suiter, tackled the nature of the digital medium and one of the most common academic uses, posting video of lectures online. Tad's video not only discussed weaknesses of online lectures, it demonstrated their shortcomings, investigated alternative modes of communicating and conveying information—especially emerging best practices in the video blogging (vlogging) community—and encouraged viewers to think about the potential for online pedagogy. As Tad wrote on his blog, *The Leisurely Historian*, "The only thing more boring than a bad lecture is a decent lecture on YouTube."[3]

In one last example from the class, "Multisensory Music Making: Unleash the Power of Music Within You!" examined a new theory of teaching and learning music: connecting visual and auditory stimuli to help musicians "connect with music on a deeper level," and "expand their range of emotional and expressive playing." A paper on this topic could not begin to capture this approach, but seeing a student play a musical phrase, tell a story about it through an image, and play it again shows how this works, transforming "expression into music."[4]

All of this argues for multimedia and visual literacy, but why *digital* storytelling?

Primarily, because it is accessible, relatively easy to teach basic technical skills, and a useful practical skill. It allows students to engage with visual and multimedia sources while researching a topic and crafting thoughtful arguments; it also creates an end product that can be shared and revised.

Several students adapted this approach to weekly assignments, submitting vlogs in place of blog postings. The blog discussion on copyright was thoughtful and lively, but Mark Bergman's vlog on the topic accomplished what a text-based blog could not. He explored the music involved in a recent copyright dispute over Coldplay's song "Viva La Vida." Guitarist Joe Satriani accused Coldplay of copyright infringement based on his 2004 song "If I Could Fly," which led to further claims of copyright infringement by the artist formerly known as Cat Stevens based on his 1973 song "Foreigner Suite." A written blog assignment could link to audio excerpts, but playing the excerpts one after the other engaged the reader/watcher in deciding whether the case had merit, creating a powerful example of the nature of copyright dispute.[5]

As Jeff McClurken likes to say, making students uncomfortable, but not paralyzed, often leads them to ask new questions, explore content more deeply, and take ownership of their learning. While this DST class experienced its fair share of technical difficulties and near disasters—more laptops died during this semester than I care to count, from natural and unnatural causes—and teaching nineteen students with various technical skills introduced its own challenges, creating ten-minute digital stories focused on historical research or on teaching and learning at the college level challenged students to think in new ways, to question not only the sources they used, but how they crafted and presented their arguments.

DST is not a silver bullet. It made students uncomfortable at different times, and for different reasons. But they all survived, emerged on the other side of the semester not only with a ten-minute digital story, but with a new appreciation for the power of iterative learning, of rethinking and questioning research, central questions, and presentation—something that doesn't always happen with essays, even at the graduate level.

Notes

1. "Tell a Story with 5 Photos for Educators," Flickr image sharing, http://www.flickr.com/groups/fivephotos/.

2. Rwany Sibaja, *Silent Voices*, http://vimeo.com/11165331.

3. *The Leisurely Historian Blog*, "Why Digital Lectures Don't Work," blog entry by Tad Suiter, May 4, 2010, http://www.leisurelyhistorian.net/why-digital-lectures-dont-work.

4. "Multisensory Music Making: Unleash the Power of Music Within You!," http://vimeo.com/11424032.

5. Mark Bergman, "Copyright Vlog," http://vimeo.com/12140910.

Assessment versus Innovation

Cathy Davidson

Most of us think that the current emphasis on assessment is a contemporary phenomenon. In fact, the rationale for testing, grading, assessing, and evaluating in a quantified fashion goes straight back to the dawn of the assembly line and the modern office; back to the beginning of education schools and business schools. If you look at most educational institutions, corporate HR departments, and government agencies today, they have adopted forms of evaluation that bear the legacy of methods designed in the early twentieth century to make evaluating the quality of people and their work as easy as inspecting a Model T as it rolls off the assembly line. The byword of the Model T is that you can have it in any color so long as its black. One size fits all. We're still judging as if we're trying to ensure that uniform, efficient sizing up of human achievement, accomplishment, effort, and productivity.

The world has changed in the last two decades, but evaluation methods have not. We have entered a new era of distributed customizable knowledge, where tasks are shared and accomplishments are iterative—in the sense that others can emend the result, that improvement is continual, and participation is the desired goal. That's how the Internet was built, and how the Firefox browser and Apache server are both sustained and maintained. Yet our prevailing methods of assessment presume nothing has changed since Ford rolled out his first automobiles, and that the goal is exactly, precisely the Model T.

More and more assessment is detached from the standard of excellence it is supposed to measure in some productive way. Because of the growing mismatch between the ways we work and learn today and the antiquated—and increasingly rigid—forms of assessment to which we subject ourselves and others, it's time for a major rethinking. At my workplace, I am required to provide an assessment of those I supervise. That's fine. But I'm also required to rank them. Since I spend the year working hard—we all do—to improve how we work together as a collaborative team, I can think of nothing more harmful to what we accomplish together than saying Person 1 is better than Person 2. That method of assessment undermines the efficiency and excellence of the team. It is also arbitrary. If I am a truly good supervisor working throughout the year to ensure that each person performs not only to his or her potential, but to the specific requirements of his or her job, I am exactly not trying to encourage my teammates to compete against one another but to, together, strive for excellence. If one member is not performing to full potential, it should be my job to say where improvement is needed, and what the path to that improvement is. It's not even relevant to specify that he or she happens not to be as good as Sarah or Johnny: that's not aiming high enough. It's simply aiming relative to our small group. That comparison happens to be gratuitous and arbitrary, relevant not to his or her job, but to who happens to work around him or her. It is destructive of management goals that, as a supervisor, I set and aspire to throughout the year.

I recently spent time with a British scholar who noted that the new government promotion and salary guidelines require that she produce four refereed articles a year. Why four? Two great ones don't mean more than four that may not be great? That's how we measure intellectual productivity? One refereed book does not count? This is a standard that is harmful to the sciences, since it says publication of those four works a year is more important than the major scientific find that might result in one hugely influential and important article in due time—not four turned out to someone else's measurement. But in her field of film studies, where a book has been long deemed more important than articles, it also means an arbitrary application of someone else's arbitrary standard to her field. It undercuts excellence in all fields.

More and more of us experience such discrepancies. The rigidity of contemporary assessment may well turn out to be a death knell. Practices often become more stringently enforced when they no longer have real utility and before they are about to be transformed or discarded. In the meantime, many of us are stuck with assessment methods that inhibit excellence, impede creativity, and serve as the antithesis to innovation. The measure may well be simple and efficient. The tragedy is that, in many cases, we have reached a binary: assessment *versus* innovation.

A Personal Cyberinfrastructure

Gardner Campbell

> Cyberinfrastructure is something more specific than the network itself, but it is something more general than a tool or a resource developed for a particular project, a range of projects, or, even more broadly, for a particular discipline.
>
> —AMERICAN COUNCIL OF LEARNED SOCIETIES, "Our Cultural Commonwealth," 2006.[1]

Sometimes progress is linear. Sometimes progress is exponential: according to the durable Moore's Law, for example, computing power doubles about every two years. Sometimes, however, progress means looping back to earlier ideas whose vitality and importance were unrecognized or underexplored at the time, and bringing those ideas back into play in a new context. This is the type of progress needed in higher education today, as students, faculty, and staff inhabit and cocreate their online lives.

The early days of the web in higher education involved workshops on basic HTML, presentations on course web pages, and seed money in the form of grants and equipment to help faculty, staff, and occasionally even students to generate and manage content in those strange "public.html" folders that suddenly appeared on newly connected desktops. Those days were exciting, but they were also difficult. Only a few faculty members had the curiosity or stamina to brave this new world. Staff time was largely occupied by keeping the system up and running, and few people understood how to bring students into this world, aside from assigning them e-mail addresses during orientation.

Then an answer seemed to appear: template-driven, plug-and-play, turn-key web applications—learning management systems—that would empower all faculty, even the most mulish Luddites, to "put their courses online." Staff could manage everything centrally, with great economies of scale and a lot more uptime. Students would have the convenience of one-stop, single-sign-on activities, from registering for classes, to participating in online discussion, to seeing grades mere seconds after they were posted.

This answer seemed to be the way forward into a world of easy-to-use affordances that would empower faculty, staff, and students without their having to learn the dreaded alphabet soup of HTML, FTP, and CSS. As far as faculty were concerned, the only letters they needed to know were L, M, S. Best of all, faculty could bring students into these environments without fear that they would be embarrassed by their lack of skill or challenged by students' unfamiliar innovations.

But that wasn't progress. It was a mere "digital facelift"—Clay Shirky's phrase for the strategies that newspapers pursued in the 1990s when they couldn't "think the unthinkable," and see that their entire world was about to change.[2] Higher education, which should be in the business of thinking the unthinkable, stood in line and bought its own version of the digital facelift. At the turn of the twenty-first century, higher education looked in the mirror and, seeing its portals, its easy-to-use LMSs, and its "digital campuses," admired itself as sleek, youthful, and attractive. But the mirror lied.

Then the web changed again: Google, Blogger, *Wikipedia*, YouTube, Facebook, and Twitter. *The medium is the message.* Higher education almost completely ignored Marshall McLuhan's central insight: new modes of communication change what can be imagined and expressed. "Any technology gradually creates a totally new human environment. Environments are not passive wrappings but active processes. . . . The 'message' of any medium or technology is the change of scale or pace or pattern that it introduces into human affairs."[3] Print is not advanced calligraphy. The web is not a more sophisticated telegraph. Yet higher education largely failed to empower the strong and effective imaginations that students need for creative citizenship in this new medium. The "progress" that higher education achieved with massive turn-key online systems, especially with the LMS, actually moved in the opposite direction. The digital facelift helped higher education deny both the needs and the opportunities emerging with this new medium.

So, how might colleges and universities shape curricula to support and inspire the imaginations that students need? Here's one idea: suppose that when students matriculate, they are assigned their own web servers—not 1-GB folders in the institution's web space, but honest-to-goodness virtualized web servers of the kind available for $7.99 a month from a variety of hosting services, with built-in affordances ranging from database maintenance to web analytics. As part of the first-year orientation, each student would pick a domain name. Over the course of the first year, in a set of lab seminars facilitated by instructional technologists, librarians, and faculty advisors from across the curriculum, students would build out their digital presences in an environment made of the medium of the web itself. They would experiment with server management tools via graphical user interfaces such as cPanel or other commodity equivalents. They would install scripts with one-click installers such as SimpleScripts. They would play with wikis and blogs; they would tinker and begin to assemble a platform to support their publishing, their archiving, their importing and exporting, their internal and external information connections. They would become, in myriad small but important ways, system administrators for their own digital lives. In short, students would build a personal cyberinfrastructure—one they would continue to modify and extend throughout their college career—and beyond.

In building that personal cyberinfrastructure, students not only would acquire crucial technical skills for their digital lives, but also would engage in work that provides richly teachable moments ranging from multimodal writing to information science, knowledge management, bibliographic instruction, and social networking. Fascinating and important innovations would emerge as students are able to shape their own cognition, learning, expression, and reflection in a digital age, in a digital medium. Students would frame, curate, share, and direct their own "engagement streams" throughout the learning environment. Like Doug Engelbart's "bootstrappers" in the Augmentation Research Center, these students would study the design and function of their digital environments, share their findings, and develop the tools for even richer and more effective metacognition, all within a medium that provides the most flexible and extensible environment for creativity and expression that human beings have ever built.

Just as the real computing revolution didn't happen until the computer became truly personal, the real IT revolution in teaching and learning won't happen until each student builds a personal cyberinfrastructure that is as thoughtfully, rigorously, and expressively composed as an excellent essay or an ingenious experiment. This vision goes beyond the personal learning environment in that it asks students to think about the web at the level of the server, with the tools and affordances that such an environment prompts and provides.[4]

Pointing students to data buckets and conduits we've already made for them won't do. Templates and training wheels may be necessary for a while, but by the time students get to college, those aids all too regularly turn into hindrances. For students who have relied on these aids, the freedom to explore and create is the last thing on their minds, so deeply has it been discouraged. Many students simply want to know what their professors want and how to give that to them. But if what the professor truly wants is for students to discover and craft their own desires and dreams, a personal cyberinfrastructure provides the opportunity. To get there, students must be effective architects, narrators, curators, and inhabitants of their own digital lives. Students with this kind of digital fluency will be well prepared for creative and responsible leadership in the post-Gutenberg age. Without such fluency, students cannot compete economically or intellectually, and the astonishing promise of the digital medium will never be fully realized.

To provide students the guidance they need to reach these goals, faculty and staff must be willing to lead by example—to demonstrate and discuss, as fellow learners, how they have created and connected their own personal cyberinfrastructures. Like the students, faculty and staff must awaken their own self-efficacy within the myriad creative possibilities that emerge from the new web. These personal cyberinfrastructures will be visible, fractal-like, in the institutional cyberinfrastructures, and the network effects that arise recursively within that relationship will allow new learning and new connections to emerge as a natural part of individual and collaborative efforts.

To build a cyberinfrastructure that scales without stifling innovation, that is self-supporting without being isolated or fatally idiosyncratic, we must start with the individual learners. Those of us who work with students must guide them to build their own personal cyberinfrastructures, to embark on their own web odysseys. And yes, we must be ready to receive their guidance as well.

Notes

1. P. N. Courant et al., "Our Cultural Commonwealth: The Report of the American Council of Learned Societies," Commission on Cyberinfrastructure for Humanities and Social Sciences, University of Southern California, 2006.

2. Clay Shirky, "Newspapers and Thinking the Unthinkable," March 13, 2009, http://www.shirky.com/weblog/2009/03/newspapers-and-thinking-the-unthinkable/.

3. Marshall McLuhan and Lewis H. Lapham, *Understanding Media: The Extensions of Man* (New York: McGraw Hill, 1964).

4. Educause Learning Initiative, "7 Things You Should Know About Personal Learning Environments," 2009, http://net.educause.edu/ir/library/pdf/ELI7049.pdf.

Voices

LEARNING MANAGEMENT SYSTEMS

Matt Gold and Jim Groom

The problem with learning management systems lies in the conjunction of three words that should not appear together. Learning is not something that can be managed via a system. We're not producing widgets here—we're attempting to inspire creative thought and critical intelligence. Learning management systems have dominated online education up until now, but must they be what we rely on in the future? Having found our way out of one box, must we immediately look for another? Can we imagine no other possibilities?

—MATT GOLD

Companies like Blackboard emerged as all-in-one solutions for managing courses online due to the relative difficulty of using the open web in the late 1990s given the unilateral nature of content delivery, limited access to the web, and the general difficulty designing and maintaining one's own space. Course-management systems fit a need. They were designed for a learning environment that posed a high threshold of difficulty for two-way participation. Yet, over the the next ten years the web became a far more conducive space for dynamic interaction and participation. At the same time, Internet penetration throughout the Western world became more and more ubiquitous, and applications that offer similar functionality as course management systems began to emerge at a fraction of the cost of centralized, proprietary systems.

So, what happens? The companies that make the learning management systems gentrify the frontier; they try and assimilate the power of these new tools within a controlled space that is safe, closed, and convenient. It is a two-pronged attack—exploiting fears about student safety along with a promise of a centralized convenience and peace of mind.

So, like the artists that moved into SoHo and the Lower East Side of New York City in the 1960s and 1970s, their pursuit of an affordable and diverse alternative to mainstream logic ultimately paves the way for capital to roll in and develop and gentrify these neighborhoods, eliminating most, if not all, of the original spaces that made them interesting and compelling to begin with.

—JIM GROOM

Hacking the Dissertation

Anastasia Salter

When I teach, I'm constantly asking my students to work in open and collaborative spaces. I prefer student work that faces outward: wikis, Twitter, blogs, game projects, etc. Like Mark Sample, I believe that the student essay is flawed—"a compressed outpouring of energy . . . that means nothing to no one."

Can't the same be said of my dissertation? To a large extent, that's even expected. The dissertation is the large work that stands as a bridge to future research. Writing it is more the process of induction: a launching point, rather than an end product. It exists, it goes in front of a committee, and mostly it is of vast significance only to the person writing it.

There are several traditional venues for feedback during the dissertation-writing process: the most common is the conference presentation, a strictly scheduled event in which a portion of the work that has presumably been tailored into a stand-alone paper. From there, draft exchanges are possible, and social media certainly has eased the exchange of these types of documents. This type of limited collaboration is a sidenote to the bulk of the writing process, which was recently satirized by the website PhD Comics as a "trip down the rabbit hole" that amounts to a personal struggle with one's research.[1]

That still hard-to-dismiss picture of the humanist surrounded by papers, not people and networks, stands in contrast to online communities where peer feedback can enhance a lonely process. The desire to share progress is seen even in tongue-in-cheek experiments like Is My Thesis Hot or Not?—a website where only the thesis statement is in play, and subject to user votes on the binary of "hot" or "not" with an open-comment system that can be an outlet for snark, or, more rarely, helpful criticism.[2]

This is one of the realities of putting work in open-access environments: it can be mocked and torn apart. More likely, it will be ignored completely. The most commonly used database for academic dissertations encourages work to be put into stasis: the ProQuest UMI Dissertation database now has an open-access model for digital publication, but the work once archived sits as a PDF and cannot evolve dynamically.[3]

There are already many projects that have experimented with open peer review and collaboration. Of those, the most successful tend to be launched by an already established academic, as with Lawrence Lessig's collective revision of his work via wiki, *Code 2.0*. Humanities dissertations have occasionally embraced dynamic digital forms: Vika Zafrin's blog, *RolandHT*, was designed for the web, and is conscious of that form in every aspect of the data and methodology. Zach Whalen's blog, *The Videogame Text*, is a working example of the dissertation text brought into an interactive space, though the stated final goal remains a traditional book proposal.[4]

In these and other cases of experimental publishing, the exclusivity of the book is being overthrown. Many grad students I've spoken with are hesitant to place their work in open access venues for fear of decreasing its value down the road: they dream—and, yes, I myself will admit to having daydreamed—of making the leap from dissertation to monograph. The reality of such leaps, of course, is that they demand transformation: take Noah Wardrip-Fruin's recent book from MIT Press, *Expressive Processing*, and compare it to his earlier dissertation of the same name.[5]

The traditional dissertation as product reflects the dominance of the book: it creates a monograph that sits in a database. The processes of the humanities are to some extent self-perpetuating: write essays as an undergraduate, conference papers as a graduate student, a dissertation as a doctoral student, and books and journal articles as a professor. Making a work open access doesn't give it an audience, just as engaging in a dynamic project and seeking community input doesn't make a work inherently valuable—but it does more seriously reflect the purposing of the dissertation as a launching point.

Perhaps as all these stages of academic production are "hacked" we'll see more dissertations embracing the models that are now experimental. I'd like to see a community form online that resembles the collaborative social networks I've made an object of study. For instance, a community like Fanfiction.net brings value to its many users not only by offering a place to share one's story, but by offering a community of collaborators—other creators of content who are enthusiastic about sharing their own knowledge and opinions because they are engaged in the same processes for themselves.[6] These types of communities go a step beyond the social networks we now have as graduate students (like Gradshare and Grad

Cafe) and become spaces that encourage continual revision, collaboration, and extension.[7] Embracing these models might bring some of the same challenges we see in the classroom, like sorting out the different values of individual authorship and dealing with the ever-present risks of plagiarism, but the results might produce dissertation work that can move more easily to relevance in a larger discourse. A dissertation written—and blogged, and revised, and remixed—in networked space need not be condemned to stasis.

Notes

1. Jorge Cham, "PhD Comics: Cecilia in Thesisland, Pt. 2: Down the Raw Bit Code," http://www.phdcomics.com/comics/archive.php?comicid=1275.

2. http://ismythesishotornot.com/.

3. "ProQuest Open Access Publishing PLUS," ProQuest, http://www.proquest.com/en-US/products/dissertations/epoa.shtml.

4. Lawrence Lessig, *Code: And Other Laws of Cyberspace, Version 2.0* (New York: Basic Books, 2006); Vika Zafrin, *RolandHT*, http://rolandht.org/; *The Videogame Text*, "Typography and Textuality: Blogging the Book Proposal," blog entry by Zach Whalen, http://www.thevideogametext.com/vgt.

5. Noah Wardrip-Fruin, *Expressive Processing: Digital Fictions, Computer Games, and Software Studies* (Cambridge, MA: MIT Press, 2012).

6. http://www.fanfiction.net/.

7. GradShare, http://www.gradshare.com/answers.html; the Grad Cafe forums—graduate school Admission, advice, discussions, help and information, http://forum.thegradcafe.com/.

How to Read a Book in One Hour

Larry Cebula

As children, we are taught that reading is always linear: you start on page one and end on page three-hundred-and-sixty-seven, and skipping pages is cheating. That is the way you read all through school, and the way most people read their whole lives. Once you get to graduate school, however, it is time to leave that childhood illusion behind.

You are no longer reading books for the stories contained inside. You are reading them for other reasons—to understand the authors' arguments, to see how they handle evidence, to examine how they structure their arguments, and to analyze their work as a whole. Perhaps above all, you need to understand how any given book fits into the theoretical landscape, how it speaks to other works on the subject, and its strengths and weaknesses. Plodding through a book one page at a time is not the best way to do this.

You need to devour books—to fall on them like a hungry weasel on a fat chicken. You break their spines, rummage about in their innards for the tasty bits, and make your way to the next chicken coop. Here is how to do it.

1. Create a clean space—a table, the book, paper, a writing utensil, and nothing else.
2. Read two academic reviews of the book, photocopied beforehand. Don't skip this step: these will tell you the book's perceived strengths and weakness. Allow five minutes for this.
3. Carefully read the introduction. A good introduction will give you the book's thesis, clues on the methods and sources, and thumbnail synopses of each chapter. Work quickly, but take good notes—with a bibliographic citation at the top of the page. Allow twenty minutes here.
4. Turn directly to the conclusion and read that. The conclusion will reinforce the thesis and have some more quotable material. In your

notes, write down one or two direct quotes suitable for using in a review or literature review, should you later be assigned to write such a beast. Allow ten–fifteen minutes here.

5. Turn to the table of contents and think about what each chapter likely contains. You may be done—in many cases in grad school the facts in any particular book will already be familiar to you; what is novel is the interpretation, and you should already have that from the introduction and conclusion. Allow five minutes here.
6. (Optional) Skim one or two of what seem to be the key chapters. Look for something clever the author has done with her or his evidence, memorable phrases, glaring weaknesses—stuff you can mention and sound thoughtful yourself when it is your turn to talk in the seminar room. Allow ten minutes, max.
7. Put the notes and photocopied review in a file folder and squirrel it away. These folders will serve as fodder for future assignments, reviews of similar books, lectures, grant applications, etc.
8. Miller time. Meet some friends and tell them the interesting things you just learned—driving it deeper into your memory.

Will you learn as much using this method as you would if you spent the five–eight hours reading it in the conventional method? Heck no. But the real meat of the book—the thesis and key points—will actually be more clear to you using this method. Otherwise it is too easy for a graduate student to get lost in the details and miss the main points.

This method works better with some books than others. If a book is considered especially important, or if it falls squarely within your research area, you should give it more time. And never, ever tell the professor that you read the assignment in an hour. Not even if that professor is me. I'll flunk you.

Hacking Institutions

The Absent Presence

A CONVERSATION

Brian Croxall and David Parry

Brian Croxall didn't have enough money to attend the annual convention of the Modern Language Association (MLA) in 2009 in Philadelphia. He was supposed to give a talk at the meeting, but instead another attendee, Sheila Cavanagh, read his candid paper about his situation to a large audience. His plight sparked widespread discussion.

The Absent Presence: Today's Faculty
—Brian Croxall

This year was to be my fourth year in a row attending MLA. I spoke in 2006, interviewed for jobs in 2007, spoke and interviewed in 2008, and had hoped to speak and interview for jobs this year as well. When the job interviews did not materialize, I made the difficult decision to not attend the convention given the financial realities of being an adjunct faculty member. I regretted not having the chance to speak—especially on a panel titled "Today's Teachers, Today's Students: Economics"—but the panel chair volunteered to deliver my paper in absentia.

I'm sorry that I can't be delivering these comments in person, and I thank Professor Cavanagh for her willingness to read them on my behalf. Hearing talks delivered by the person who did not write them is only slightly better than having to be the person who is reading a talk she didn't write, so I'll be brief. At the same time, however, I can think of no more appropriate way for me to give a talk in a panel titled "Today's Students, Today's Teachers: Economics" than in this manner.

After all, I'm not a tenure-track faculty member, and the truth of the matter is that I simply cannot afford to come to this year's MLA. I know that we as a profession are increasingly aware of the less than ideal conditions under which contingent faculty members—and graduate students—labor while providing more than half of the instruction that undergraduates receive across the nation: a fact that the *Chronicle of Higher Education* and other publications have reported on frequently.[1] If we are talking about "today's teachers," then more of them look like me—at least in a professional sense—than look like the people who will be on the dais at the presidential address later on this evening. That means that most of the students in America are also taught by people that are like me. In a very real sense, I—and the people situated in a similar professional and economic quandary—are today's teachers of today's students. And for the most part, we're not at the MLA this year.

Again, I'm not at the MLA this year because it's not economically feasible. I had hoped to be here for job interviews—as well as to speak as a member of this panel discussion. This was my third year on the job market, and I applied to every job in North America that I was even remotely qualified for: all forty-one of them. Unfortunately, I did not receive any interviews, despite having added two articles accepted by peer-reviewed journals, five new classes, and several new awards and honors to my curriculum vitae. According to my records, applying to those forty-one jobs cost me $257.54. I was prepared to pay the additional expenses of attending the MLA—$125 for registration, $279.20 for a plane ticket, approximately $180 for lodging with a roommate: a total of $584.20—out of pocket so that I could have a chance of getting one of those forty-one jobs. I was even luckier than most faculty—remember, most of today's faculty are contingent—in that my institution was willing to provide me with $200 support to attend conferences throughout the academic year. But once it became apparent that I wasn't going to be having any interviews, I could no longer justify the outlay of $400 out of a salary that puts me only $1,210 above the 2009 Federal poverty guidelines. (And yes, that means I do qualify for food stamps while working a full-time job as a professor!)

I can't imagine that I'm alone in this dilemma of not attending this year's convention due to finances and the anemic job market. After all, as the *New York Times* reported on December 17, 2009, the number of listings in the MLA's job information list was down 37 percent from 2008's numbers—the sharpest decline since MLA started tracking job ads in 1974. It's not like 2008 was a banner year, however. The listings a year ago were down 26 percent from what they had been in 2007.[2]

Landing a job in the professoriate has been difficult for well more than this decade, but the recent economic crisis has necessitated—or allowed, if we're feeling cynical—administrators trimming budgets so that less and less tenure-track faculty are hired. What this means is that more and more contingent faculty are employed to teach the increasing number of students who are matriculating at the nation's universities. So . . . perhaps it's not that employment is going down for humanists with the PhD. Rather, it is sustainable employment that is evaporating. (I'm looking at you, California.) After all, the demand for contingent faculty labor will probably rise sharply as the number of students enrolling in colleges rises due to the nation's recent economic crisis. Since we can't expect other schools to be as generous as mine with travel funds to contingent faculty, there should be fewer and fewer faculty members at the MLA in the future because less and less of the nation's faculty will be able to afford to get here.

"But"—the administrators say—"the MLA is only a conference, one where people read papers at each other. What difference does it make whether you attend or not?" Such questions are of course misleading since it's not as if my department is willing to give me more money to travel to other conferences *instead* of the MLA. So the problem of not being able to afford to attend the MLA is really the problem of attending *any* conference, other than a local one. And attending conferences is critical for one's scholarship since it allows one to hear the latest research in one's field. I especially appreciate how large the MLA is since I can find opportunities to attend panels that represent the full 150 years of American literature that my research covers. Attending this conference—or others—keeps me abreast of the latest scholarship, and helps me produce scholarship that pushes the state of my fields forward. As one of today's teachers, attending conferences helps me be more prepared to teach today's students these new developments, preparing them to be more effective readers of literature, whether they are English or biostatistics majors. Moreover, it is at conferences that I am most likely to have the opportunity to meet with old and new colleagues whose work intersects most closely with my own. Schools only need so many Shakespeare scholars; not so the MLA! Yet attending conferences isn't just about seeing old friends; the relationships formed with colleagues at conferences again help us produce scholarship. For example, the panel that I spoke on last year has resulted in a book-length collaboration among the four panelists, none of whom had met previously. When the majority of faculty—who are, again, contingent faculty—cannot attend the MLA, or any other conference, it results in a faculty that cannot advance; that does not, in other words, appear to be doing the things that would warrant their conversion to the tenure track. Our placement as contingent faculty quickly becomes a self-fulfilling event.

But having a faculty majority comprised of contingent faculty means a lot more than just conferences being less and less attended. In my case, it means that my students cannot easily meet with me for office hours since contingent faculty don't really have offices. It means that they do not get effective, personal mentoring because I have too many students. It means that I cannot give the small and frequent assignments that I believe teach them more than a "three-paper class" because I do not have time to grade ninety students' small and frequent assignments. It means that the courses they can take from me will not be updated as frequently as I think is ideal because I will be spending all of my spare time looking for more secure employment—or working a part-time job. In other words, when we shortchange (pun intended) today's teachers—the majority of us who are, finally and for the last time, contingent and not present at this year's MLA—we simultaneously shortchange today's students. And those students will be that much less likely to become literature professors in the future. Why should they? It's not currently a sustainable profession; but even more so, they will have had that many fewer chances to have those interactions with teachers that lead to today's students wanting to become tomorrow's teachers.

Be Online or Be Irrelevant: Brian Croxall, the MLA, and Social Media

—David Parry

One of the much talked-about items at this year's MLA was Brian Croxall's paper, or nonpaper, titled, "The Absent Presence: Today's Faculty." I say nonpaper because Brian, who is currently on the job market and an adjunct faculty, didn't attend the MLA; instead, he published his paper to his own website. For several reasons, Brian's paper hit a nerve. Indeed the *Chronicle of Higher Education* picked up the story—a piece which for a few days was listed as the most popular story on the *Chronicle*'s website.[3] His paper became, arguably, the most talked-about paper of the convention.

In part, Brian's story is a story of the rise of social media and its influence. If you imagined asking all of the MLA attendees, not just the social-media enabled ones, what papers/talks/panels were influential, my guess is that Brian's might not make the list, or if it did, it wouldn't top the list. That is because most of the chatter about the paper was taking place online, not in the space of the MLA.

Let's be honest, at any given session you are lucky if you get over 50 attendees; assuming the panel Brian was supposed to be on was well attended, maybe 100 people actually heard his paper being read. But, the real influence of Brian's paper can't be measured this way. The real influence should be measured by how many people read his paper who didn't attend the MLA. According to Brian, views to his blog jumped 200–300 percent in the two days following his post; even being conservative one could guess that over 2,000 people performed more than a cursory glance at his paper. Brian tells me that in total, since the convention, there have probably been close to 5,000 unique views. 5,000 people: that is half the size of the convention.

So, if you asked all academics across the United States who were following the MLA—reading the *Chronicle,* following academic websites and blogs—what the most influential story out of MLA was, I think Brian's would have topped the list, easily. Most academics would perform serious acts of defilement to get a readership in the thousands, and Brian got it overnight.

Or, not really . . . Brian built that readership over the last three years.

As Amanda French argues on her blog, what social media affords us is the opportunity to amplify scholarly communication.[4] As she points out in her analysis (interestingly enough, Amanda was not at MLA, but she was still tweeting about the MLA during the conference), only 3 percent of the people at MLA were tweeting about it. Compare that to other conferences, even other academic ones, and this looks rather pathetic. Clearly MLAers have a long way to go in coming to terms with social media as a place for scholarly conversation.

What made Brian's paper so influential/successful is that Brian had already spent a great deal of time building network capital. He was one of the first people I followed on Twitter, and was one of the panelists at last year's MLA-Twitter panel. He teaches with technology. I know several professors who borrow/steal his assignments. I personally looked at his class wiki when designing my own. Besides having a substantial traditional CV, Brian has a lot of street cred in the digital humanities/social-networking/academic world. More than a lot of folks, and deservedly so. It isn't that he just "plays" with all this social media, he actually contributes to the community of scholars who are using it, in ways that are recognized as meaningful and important.

In this regard, I couldn't disagree with Bitch Ph.D. more—someone with whom I often agree—when she claims on her blog that, "Professor Croxall is, if I may, a virtual nobody."[5]

Not true. Unlike Bitch Ph.D., he is not anonymous, or even pseudo-anonymous; his online identity and real-world identity are the same. He is far from a virtual nobody. Indeed, I would say he is one of the more prominent voices on matters digital and academia. He is clearly a "*virtual* somebody," and he has made himself a "virtual somebody" by being an active, productive, important, member of the "virtual academic community." If he is anything he is a "*real* nobody," but a "*virtual* somebody." In the digital world, network capital is the real coin of the realm, and Brian has a good bit of it, which when mustered and amplified through the network capital of others (Kathleen Fitzpatrick, Dan Cohen, Amanda French, Matt Gold, and Chuck Tryon—all of us tweeted about Brian's piece), brings him more audience members than he could ever really hope to get in one room at the MLA.

Therefore, Brian isn't a "virtual nobody," and he isn't a "potential somebody"—he is a scholar of the digital humanities—one that ought to be recognized. But here is the disconnect. Brian has a lot of coin in the realm of network capital, but this hasn't yielded any coin in the realm of brick-and-mortar institutions. If we were really seeing the rise of the digital humanities, someone like Brian wouldn't be without a job, and the fact that he published his paper online wouldn't be such an oddity; it would be standard practice. Instead, Brian's move seems, in the words of Bitch Ph.D., "all meta- and performative and shit"—when in fact it is what scholars should be doing. The fact that a prominent digital scholar like Brian doesn't even get one interview at the MLA means more than the economy is bad, that tenure-track jobs are not being offered, but rather that universities are still valuing the wrong stuff. They are looking for "real somebodies" instead of "virtual somebodies."

This is the brilliance of Brian's paper, content not withstanding: he made his material more relevant than all the other papers that weren't published, he engaged the outside—even if it was a paper that was a lot of inside baseball on the workings of the academy—because he opened his analysis and thinking to a wider audience, and as Amanda French and Bitch Ph.D. remark, did it with a real-time spin that enhanced the level of content and delivery. The real influence should be measured by how many people read his paper who didn't attend the MLA. Or maybe, the real influence of his paper should be measured by how many nonacademics read his paper. Scholars need to be online or be irrelevant, because our future depends upon it, but more importantly, the future of how knowledge production and dissemination takes place in the broader culture will be determined by it.

Reflections on Going Viral at the MLA
—Brian Croxall

Recently, I've had to come to grips with the fact that I've quite likely peaked. The paper that I was supposed to read at the 2009 Modern Language Association's convention went viral.

When I chose at the last minute not to attend the conference, given my lack of job interviews, insufficient travel funds, and the low salary of a visiting professor, I rewrote the paper that I had planned to present at a panel on "Today's Students, Today's Teachers: Economics" to talk about "The Absent Presence" of people who, like me, could not afford to attend conferences. I sent it to the panel chair to read on my behalf, posted it to my blog, and mentioned on Twitter that I had done so. The result was shocking. Within twenty-four hours, some 2,000 people had read my paper, spurred in no small part by an article in the *Chronicle of Higher Education*, a blog post by the anonymous academic blogger Bitch Ph.D., and countless mentions on Twitter and other blogs. By the end of the convention, my blog had received over 7,000 page views.

The scope of going viral became more apparent when I returned to campus a week later, for the start of the semester, to discover that every colleague I ran into had read the piece. Instead of being heard by a small group of people who attended the panel at which I was to speak, my paper had been read by more people—and colleagues!—than I could ever reasonably expect to read any article or book that I might write in the future. So there it is: I've had my fifteen minutes.

It's a compelling narrative: A "virtual nobody," as Bitch Ph.D. put it, comes out of nowhere, takes one of the biggest academic conferences by storm, and gets noticed by thousands. He rides off triumphantly into the sunset and even gets to write a follow-up for the *Chronicle*. But if there's one thing that I learned in graduate school, it's that every narrative can—and probably should, if you're looking to get published—get deconstructed. On reflection, it seems to me worthwhile to explore one thing that was said about my paper, and one thing that was repeatedly said to me about my paper.

First is the suggestion that my paper was, as the *Chronicle* put it, possibly the "most-talked-about presentation" at the conference. But let's be honest: The number of people talking about my paper in Philadelphia could only have been very small. After all, the chair informs me that there were approximately thirty-five people who attended the panel. Far more people certainly attended Catherine Porter's presidential address and discussed her call to reconsider the importance of translations and those who create them. My paper could not have been anything more than a blip on the conversational radar. It seems certain that practically no one at the real MLA was talking about my paper. How could they have? They hadn't heard it.

Instead, my paper and the response it generated happened at a virtual MLA. I'm not talking about a conference taking place in Second Life, but rather the real-time supplement to the physical conference that was conducted via social-media tools. The crowd presenting at the virtual MLA was considerably smaller than the approximately 7,400 scholars who came to Philadelphia. For example, Amanda French estimated that only 256 people used Twitter with the official #mla09 hashtag, based on data from the tweet-storage service TwapperKeeper. And while it's nearly impossible to tell how many people blogged about the MLA, one can reasonably assume that they were fewer than those using Twitter, since participation on Twitter takes less time than blogging.

But if the number of those participating in the virtual MLA was so much smaller, how did so many people read my paper? The difference is that it is only the number of people presenting at the virtual MLA that is small; the audience is much, much larger. The virtual MLA requires no registration fee or travel, and when you lower those bars via social media, anyone can attend. That includes not only people like me, who couldn't afford the real MLA, but also scholars from outside the field of literary studies. My website's views really started spiking when my paper was tweeted by two historians: Dan Cohen, Director of the Roy Rosenzweig Center for History and New Media at George Mason University, and Jo Guldi, a junior fellow at the Harvard Society of Fellows. But it's not only people without funds to travel or academics outside the field who attend the virtual MLA; it really can be anyone. Curious onlookers who might want to know what exactly it is that literature professors do can suddenly find out; it is that group that caused my paper to go viral.

The virtual MLA suggests a few things about humanities scholarship in the twenty-first century. First, scholarship will be freely accessible online. Online scholarship not only is the next logical step for publication, but also presents a way to address an expanding audience. The much-discussed crisis in the humanities has at its origin the question of what—if anything—the humanities are good for. It has been difficult to answer that question, in part because our scholarship is frequently inaccessible, published in small journals, or contained in subscription-only databases. Making our work freely accessible—whether in open-access journals or on our own websites—means that more people will be able to see what we are doing. While I'm not naive enough to think that access alone will make people see why the study of film or history matters, it seems certain that, as David Parry—an assistant professor of emerging media and communications at the University of Texas at Dallas—recently put it, humanities scholars must "be online or be irrelevant."

Second, scholarship in the age of the virtual MLA will become increasingly collaborative and participatory. We all know that collaboration in the humanities is made difficult by institutional pressures associated with tenure and promotion. Moving scholarship online lowers some other practical barriers to collaboration. Moreover, cooperation will not only be with our colleagues down the hall. We need to be ready to work with knowledgeable hobbyists—aka independent scholars—and to share credit with those partners. We may find that the focus of our work shifts a bit in response to engagement with people outside academia. And, again, we may find that what we as humanities scholars do will be better understood and valued.

Let me extract myself from the unlikely role of futurist and focus on what was said to me in the days following my paper's going viral. In blog comments, on Twitter, via e-mail messages, and even in real life, people repeatedly told me that they hoped the exposure I was receiving would lead to some new career opportunities for me. I naturally appreciated such wishes, and must confess to having thought something similar myself.

But upon further reflection, I think that such hopes—mine included—miss the point of my paper.

What caught people's attention was not so much my personal experience, but rather how it reflected that of an ever-increasing portion of today's faculty members. While I would certainly like to have more secure employment, the conversion of just one person from contingent faculty to the tenure track will not change any of the conditions that prevented me and other members of the new faculty majority from attending the MLA conference. Naturally, almost everyone who wished me well would have expressed similar thoughts to the rest of the nation's non-tenure-track faculty members had they the venue to do so. I found myself wondering, then, if my paper really had put me in the position of an Everyman, as the *Chronicle* suggested. Were the calls for someone to do something for Brian Croxall reflective of a faint hope that saving Everyman could result in saving the entire profession?

As wonderful as it would be for the wasteland of academic career opportunities to be saved by the revivification of some Eliotic Adjunct King, it just can't work that way. The problems of contingent academic labor are systemic, and perhaps cannot be adequately addressed by a single department or even a university, let alone the blogosphere.

But one solution is to make sure that those who are applying to graduate school know very, very clearly what they are getting into. No one at my undergraduate alma mater told me in 2001 about the realities of the job market, and it certainly wasn't in the interest of the university that accepted me for graduate study to do so. If we humanists want to be humane, we ought to level with our undergraduates.

By chance, I just received an e-mail message from someone who attended my college and is interviewing as a candidate in my graduate department. She wanted to know what she could do to prepare. What did I do? I answered her questions as best I could. I also pointed her to several articles by Thomas H. Benton in the *Chronicle* that outline the risks of graduate school in the humanities, and I mentioned a paper by Brian Croxall. That guy may have peaked, but he made a good point.

Note

1. For example, Audrey Williams June, "Nearly Half of Undergraduate Courses Are Taught by Non-Tenure-Track Instructors," *Chronicle of Higher Education*, December 3, 2008, http://chronicle.com/article/Non-Tenure-Track-Instructors/1380/.

2. Tamar Lewin, "At Colleges, Humanities Job Outlook Gets Bleaker," *New York Times*, December 18, 2009, http://www.nytimes.com/2009/12/18/education/18professor.html.

3. Jennifer Howard, "Missing in Action at the MLA: Today's Teachers of Today's Students," *Chronicle of Higher Education*, December 29, 2009, http://chronicle.com/article/Missing-in-Action-at-the-ML/63276/.

4. *Amandafrench.net*, "Make '10'; Louder, or, the Amplification of Scholarly Communication," blog entry by Amanda French, December 30, 2009, http://amandafrench.net/blog/2009/12/30/make-10-louder/.

5. *Bitch Ph.D.*, "Auld Lang Syne," December 29, 2009, http://bitchphd.blogspot.com/2009/12/auld-lang-syne.html.

Uninvited Guests

TWITTER AT INVITATION-ONLY EVENTS

Bethany Nowviskie

Invitation-only gatherings are often designed as specific interventions in a certain scene or subdiscipline, and therefore a lot of care goes into identifying and recruiting participants who are either positioned to make a desired intellectual contribution to the immediate proceedings, or to synthesize and take the work of a group forward after the lights go out in the auditorium. Other events are imagined as learning experiences or sites for advanced training, and participants may be identified—and excluded—based on level of need, or on the relative merit of their applications to attend.

Organizers know—and generally regret—that pragmatic concerns and financial constraints result in the exclusion of a multitude of interesting people and perspectives. Closed events are not crafted with the goal of keeping "the wrong people" out, but of bringing enough—or, more accurately, a manageable number—of the right people in. These things need to be worth the investments they require, both of funds—often quite scarce for humanities undertakings—and other "costs of opportunity," including the work the organizing group is therefore not engaged in, and the invaluable time and energy of all participants.

But goal-oriented, laser-like focus and a predetermined guest list naturally put an event in danger of over-determined—predictable, excessively conservative, even tedious—conversations and outcomes. This is a risk of which good organizers are conscious, and against which they press. The most common way to work within attendance constraints and still leave a crack in the door is to think of invited participants as ambassadors of certain communities. Many symposium attendees will adopt a representative stance even without being asked to, as soon as they realize that they are the only—whatever: literary theorist/material-culture expert/digital historian/etc.—in the room. And some moderators will make desired personae explicit. (I use that word deliberately, because this kind of representation is necessarily masquerade, and no one seriously thinks it compensates for absence—however, ritual and performative aspects of academic interaction are often particularly highlighted at smallish events.)

At the same time, there's room elsewhere to ramble, and ways to include a broader set of voices. Traditional professional-society meetings are rarely closed, but typically finance "openness" through membership and conference fees and—often—by sacrificing the degree of attention to product and coherence that can be paid at a smaller, more carefully crafted gathering. Or you could build your own conference, on the fly. In our *DIY U*, Edupunk era, we're experiencing an explosion of "unconferences." The premier model in the humanities is THATCamp (The Humanities and Technology Camp), which originated at the Roy Rosenzweig Center for History and New Media at George Mason University. This is a do-it-yourself digital humanities conference, at which a hat is passed for donations, only the loosest practicable vetting of attendees is done, and participants collaboratively set the discussion and demonstration agenda at an opening session and "vote with their feet" thereafter; that is to say, they take continual responsibility for their own conference experience by freely floating—at any point—to other scheduled sessions or spontaneously creating new sessions that strike them as more useful. (Some of my most productive and stimulating professional experiences of the past few years have taken place at unconferences.) Many events are now streaming passive audio and video live, and experimenting with venues like Second Life as substitutes for the expense of physical presence and embodied interaction. In the past year, I have even unexpectedly "attended" an event or two that combined live streaming with the DIY sensibility, when a local participant realized the proceedings would be of interest to a larger group, called out, "Anybody mind if I broadcast this?," and set up a spontaneous Ustream.

And then there's the pervasiveness of Twitter. The litany of invitation-only gatherings in my second paragraph had associated Twitter hashtags, which are themselves a public invitation to aggregate perspectives and join in conversation. A hashtag is a small piece of metadata, agreed upon by Twitter users informally—by virtue of collective use—as an appropriate marker for a particular concept or moment. Some hashtags are jokes, some are prayer beads, some are signifiers for emerging perspectives and nascent online communities (see #alt-ac, the hashtag for discussions of alternative academic careers), and some mark Twitter messages as relevant to the discussion at a conference or other event.[1] Twitter has played an important and occasionally transformative role at every academic gathering I have attended since early 2008. It has provided useful—and sometimes surprising—demonstrations, for conference and meeting participants, of the engagement of broad and underrepresented communities with issues under debate. It has brought divergent perspectives helpfully into play, sharpening discussion, and leading to proposals with broader reach and impact. In a time of dwindling travel budgets, it has allowed key, already well-networked community members to participate in meetings from afar, with little technical overhead and less disruption to their working lives than formal, virtual participation would require through an interface like Second Life.

Twitter also allows invited conference goers to spread a wealth of ideas being voiced behind closed doors. These ideas are shared with established but evolving networks, which—at the conferences I attend, but each one is different—largely consist of students and colleagues in higher education, and in the worlds of academic publishing; libraries; museums and archives; information technology; and humanities centers, labs, and institutes. I have seen Twitter use at academic conferences promote valuable exchange among university and K–12 educators, and contribute to and demonstrate value in the public humanities in an immediate and tangible way. If Twitter itself—as commonly used by academics—operates as a gift economy, then conference hashtags are little beacons of that generosity.

But it's not all sunny in closed-conference-open-Twitter land.

There are two conflicting tensions, which are commonly expressed by both sets of my interlocutors—sometimes even simultaneously—in online and face-to-face communications during private conferences. The voice from Twitter cries: "Elitism! Hypocrisy! How can you be discussing—pick your poison: the public humanities, the future of scholarly communication, the changing nature of the disciplines—in a cloister? Who are these privileged few? And why weren't we all invited to attend?" To be fair: in my experience, messages of thanks to those who have tweeted, for broadcasting the ideas of the gathering to a wider audience, far outweigh any complaints—but a strident complaint or two, often from colleagues from sadly under-funded institutions, is invariably present. It is to the complaining Twitterati that I have addressed my long preamble on the aims and necessary limitations of smaller gatherings. Sorry, guys—really. It's usually about the money and the focus, but sometimes it's even because they couldn't manage to book a larger room.

And of course my lengthy disquisition on Twitter was meant to level the playing field for those senior colleagues—yes, this divide is largely generational—who have not engaged with Twitter, and who have indicated to me how troubling they find its use in academic settings. For it is the anti-Twitter reproach from within the conference room that I most want to address.

I suspect conference followers and participants on Twitter—whose presence Margaret Atwood likens to "having fairies at the bottom of your garden"—have no idea how magically disruptive they are. If they sense it, they may still be surprised at the character of that disruption. Several times now, I have heard the technology the Twitter community embraces and explicitly figures as democratizing and personalizing described in terms of alienation, invasion, and exclusion. These face-to-face conversations about Twitter are so fraught that delicacy cannot accord with 140-character limitations, and therefore they do not make it into the online record. Sometimes, indeed, they only come in a private, kindly meant word over drinks, or in shared taxicabs after the tweeting has ceased. Other times, it gets heated and publicly awkward.

Five problems with Twitter use at closed gatherings have been expressed to me.

The first is dismay that its application was not evident to everyone from the outset of the event. A small group of us deliberately heightened this response at a recent gathering, when we decided to "pull the curtain" on a hashtagged Twitter conversation that had been going on unnoticed by the majority of the fairly traditional scholarly crowd. The criticism is fair; that Twitter changes a conference dynamic in ways that may be invisible to some participants. The possibility of its presence probably should be addressed at the outset of closed conferences for a little while, in order that any requested ground rules can be discussed and agreed upon, and to make participants aware of the option to engage. Some professional societies, such as the Modern Language Association, and membership organizations, such as the Coalition for Networked Information, have begun promoting Twitter hashtags or even publicizing them well ahead of a conference event. Regardless, you can basically assume that if people have open laptops or handheld devices at a gathering, and still seem alert, they're note-taking or tweeting—not reading email or playing games. At least, not much.

The second issue is related: a feeling that Twitter use is exclusionary. At the outset of a closed conference, some people may have access to it, and others may not. I have figured Twitter as a democratizing medium; however, participation in it is not universal. For most people in academic settings, this is a choice. Because accounts are free and easy to set up, the only reason you can't rapidly remedy the problem, if you wish to, is that you may lack a laptop or smartphone. When you first set up your account—especially if you do so in the middle of a rapid-fire exchange—you are likely to be a little inept and lost. This is a sinking feeling you might recall from your early days of graduate school, or your first academic conference. It passes quickly, as you learn the lingo and cultural codes.

Next comes the concern that Twitter damages one's ability to engage and converse in the room, or that it lowers the level of discourse. Attentional demands may be a problem for some, as Twitter use is a learned skill. As to the latter issue, I will address only deliberate rudeness, because I worry that statements about lowered discourse are simply code for "discourse with people not like me," and suspect that no arguments of mine will shake the foundations of that view. New-media scholar danah boyd and others have exposed rudeness in backchannel chatter as a real concern, with immediate and dreadful implications for speakers at popular conferences.[2] However, it is important to say that Twitter use does not inherently promote inattention or bad behavior.

I've never witnessed a nasty backchannel in an academic setting—where we generally do share notions of fairness and propriety. More frequently, there's a little lag between the themes expressed in a Twitter conversation and the topics being discussed in the room, which can cause participants to divide their attention, but which can also evolve as an interesting counterpoint to later discussions.

Privacy concerns related to Twitter use at closed gatherings are a real issue. Often the greatest virtue of an invitation-only event, for participants who represent administrative units or high-profile organizations, is the opportunity to speak a little more candidly than they can in public. In my experience, Twitter users are sensitive to these moments and either moderate their observations and reportage accordingly or refrain from tweeting at all. If, as it seems, we are moving into a period in which always-on, networked communication becomes the norm, even at private academic events, it is the responsibility of participants to remain sensitive to desires for confidentiality or discretion—and, in the moment, speakers may need to make these desires a little more plain.

Finally, the need for privacy is not the same as a wish for control. I am fairly unsympathetic to an ownership frustration I have heard from a small number of scholars, manifesting as a desire that ideas they express at conferences—even well attributed—not be circulated via Twitter. I have come to understand that this concern stems less from a kind of proprietary interest over the ideas—that is to say, it is less a matter akin to copyright—than from a sensation of the loss of control. The level of control we used to feel over the distribution and reception of scholarly statements was only ever an illusion made possible by the small scale and relative snail's pace of print publication. It was also enabled by authority systems that—while they have performed a salutary function of filtering and quality assurance—are under scrutiny in an age of electronic text, because of their incongruence, economic instability, and cumulatively stifling effect.

One manifestation of this lack of control is the acknowledged "telephone game" of Twitter—the degree to which repetition with a difference can lead to partial or missed understandings. Sometimes, offhand, minor points that slip right past the sanctioned, face-to-face conversation can make it big online: that's human interaction for you. The Twittering fingers tweet, and having tweeted, twitter on; or live blog, or take notes in wikis, et cetera. Although it can be helpful when speakers are plugged in enough to be able to influence conversation in both offline and online streams—not even necessarily simultaneously—it is simply folly to think that we can control what's being said about us on the Internet. That was never what scholarly communication was about, anyway.

I'd offer three strategies to address concerns about the immediacy of web publishing of conference proceedings via Twitter.

The first is something we're always doing anyway: simply working to express our ideas as clearly as possible in the room, and to listen actively for feedback that may suggest misunderstanding or lack of conveyed nuance. Good luck with that (sincerely!).

Perhaps a more implementable suggestion for speakers and conference participants concerned about these matters is that they publicly request their names not be attached to tweets or blog posts. This strikes me as most valid when it touches on issues of privacy and confidentiality—but be aware that when your name is used on Twitter, it is likely done in an innocent spirit of attribution. If your ideas are cited, chances are good that the writer approves of them and wishes to lend you a microphone—or at least that he or she thought your statements interesting and worthy of further discussion. If, on the other hand, your perspective is represented in a critical way and you are cited as its source, it's probably because you are known to be on Twitter and presumed to be as able to defend yourself there as elsewhere. In other words, I have heard some anxiety expressed about personal attack, but—while contentious conversations have been opened up on Twitter in a familiar spirit of academic debate—I cannot recall ever seeing a specific, much less ad hominem, hostile response to a colleague who lacks a presence on Twitter, or might be thought defenseless in that medium. There's not a lot of passive aggression in an environment that trades on professional identity, necessarily precise language, clear attribution, and open exchange.

Most of what I've said is relevant to public as well as invitation-only academic events—but the turmoil around conference use of Twitter over the past year has seemed most acute at private gatherings. It clearly relates to the ethos of the academic Twitter demographic—mostly consisting of tech-savvy, early-career scholars or #alt-ac professionals—and the expectations and longstanding traditions that inhere in private events. Invitation-only meetings often involve more established scholars and administrators who have put in their dues under a very different set of academic protocols and for whom networked communication is important, but not necessarily ever-present.

These groups need to find ways to move forward together within the new norms of scholarly communication, and in a way that enhances shared work and promotes meaningful interconnectedness. Which brings me to the final strategy I'd suggest we all adopt: simply to—or continue to—participate.

Notes

1. http://www.twapperkeeper.com/hashtag/alt-ac. Also see http://www.twapperkeeper.com/hashtag/reenx and http://tagdef.com/uvashape. Each of these references will—depending on the ebb and flow of networked conversation—lead you to current or archived tweets stemming from a referenced gathering, or maybe even indicate to you that nobody has been chatting under a particular rubric lately. I've taken a variety of approaches in these references to demonstrate a few ways of accessing Twitter conversations and highlight the degree to which tweets are both ephemeral in that they are part of a fairly volatile landscape of protocols and interfaces, and capturable, as part of our cultural record. Whatever you see when going to those links is unlikely to be what I saw when I chose to publish them here—and it's not unlikely that a link or two will break. However, the Twitter backchannel conversation for at least one of those conferences (#uvashape) is to be published by Rice University Press. Also, the Library of Congress has announced

an initiative to archive the entire Twitter corpus—an amazing resource for future scholars. *Library of Congress Blog*, "How Tweet It Is!: Library Acquires Entire Twitter Archive," blog entry by Matt Raymond, April 4, 2010, http://blogs.loc.gov/loc/2010/04/how-tweet-it-is-library-acquires-entire-twitter-archive/.

2. *danah boyd: apophenia*, "Spectacle at Web2.0 Expo . . . from My Perspective," blog entry by danah boyd, November 24, 2009, http://www.zephoria.org/thoughts/archives/2009/11/24/spectacle_at_we.html.

Unconferences

Ethan Watrall, James Calder, Jeremy Boggs

Notes on Organizing an Unconference

—Ethan Watrall

While the term "unconference" has been applied—or self-applied—to a wide variety of events, it usually refers to a lightly organized conference in which the attendees themselves determine the schedule. In most cases, unconferences attempt to avoid the traditional unidirectional paper model in favor of meaningful and productive conversations around democratically agreed upon topics—organized into sessions. Unconferences traditionally have low registration fees, and therefore run on a much more conservative budget, compared to more traditional meetings or conferences. The other thing that sets unconferences apart from traditional conferences is that they usually have far fewer attendees: it is not uncommon for unconferences to be attended by no more than 75–100 people.

Despite the fact that the unconference idea got its start—and is still going very strong—in the tech sphere, at events like BarCamp, Foo Camp, and BloggerCon, they are becoming increasingly popular in the scholarly landscape. This is no great surprise as many scholars are beginning to feel that traditional academic conferences and meetings are perhaps not as productive as they once were. In addition, in today's economic climate (with many departments reducing, or even completely removing, travel funds), the financial burden—including the often high cost of registration—of a traditional conference has made it impossible for many scholars to attend more than one or two conferences in their domain, or perhaps none at all. Hence, the often very low registration fees of an unconference make them quite appealing.

I'm not saying there isn't a place for traditional conferences in academia. They are important for a lot of reasons—not the least of all being part of the tenure and promotion machine. However, unconferences fill an extremely important niche in the scholarly ecosystem. It is worth noting that several traditional conferences are planning on experimenting, or have already experimented, with unconference sessions—essentially, an unconference within a conference.

I have been very fortunate to co-organize Great Lakes THATCamp (a regional version of The Humanities and Technology Camp), and found it one of the most rewarding and exciting things I've ever done. As such, there were some things that I learned during the process which might prove useful to those adventurous souls who are thinking about organizing their own unconference—either as a stand-alone event, or as part of a traditional conference.

"Lightly Organized" Doesn't Mean No Organization

Just because an unconference doesn't have the organizational and logistical trappings of a traditional conference—lengthy paper submission/acceptance cycle, mind-boggling schedule, detailed conference program, and complete conference abstracts—doesn't mean that a lot of work doesn't go into making sure they are organized well. I was quite surprised by the number of colleagues—people unfamiliar with the unconference model—who, upon hearing that I was co-organizing Great Lakes THATCamp, said something akin to "well, I guess that means you don't have a lot to do." Nothing could be further from the truth. If an unconference is to be done right, it's not just a matter of getting some rooms, setting a date, and spreading the word. "Light organization" is an art unto itself. There are things that need to be organized and controlled—there is absolutely no doubt about that. However, you can't step over the line into over-organization, and try to control every little bit of the event.

A Venue that Facilitates Conversation

One of the most important hallmarks of an unconference are meaningful and productive conversations—whether they take place in large groups, small groups, or between two or three attendees. As such, unconference organizers should do their best to arrange a venue that facilitates these kinds of conversations. If you can manage it, a venue with a variety of room types and sizes is great. If all you can manage are classrooms—which might be the case if your unconference is taking place on a university campus—try to to get rooms where the chairs/desks aren't bolted to the ground. This allows the attendees to reconfigure the space as they see fit. If you are able, also try to find a venue that has smaller, informal conversation spaces as well. Conference rooms are great for this. Don't discount two or three comfortable chairs—or even benches—strewn hither and yon in hallways and corners. Anywhere where people can hang out comfortably during the day and have meaningful conversations.

Remember, An Unconference Isn't About You

An unconference is as much about the participants themselves as it is about you. You might have organized the event, but it doesn't belong to you. As such, you need to make sure that, whenever possible, decisions are made by the attendees themselves. In many ways, each attendee should be seen as much of an organizer as you.

Be Flexible

This is easily the most important thing I learned when organizing Great Lakes THATCamp: be flexible. Flexibility and fluidity is the name of the game at an unconference. Attempting to control every aspect of the event with an iron fist will probably end up in disaster. If the participants want to change the overall schedule on the fly, let them—remember, the participants are as much in charge as you are. If participants decide to change the topic of a particular session midway through, don't raise a fuss. If you need to push lunch forward so that the momentum of a particularly fruitful and exciting session can continue, do so. If the way in which you planned on building the initial schedule isn't working out, figure out a better way, and don't be afraid to ask the attendees themselves.

The Bottom Line

The subtext of all of these thoughts is that you should never forget that the conversations between attendees drive an unconference. You need to do everything you can to facilitate these conversations.

Getting the Most Out of an Unconference
—James Calder

Over the past couple of years, I have been fortunate enough to be able to attend several unconferences, both locally and nationally. I say fortunate because these experiences have opened my eyes to how amazing the unconference format can be. I cannot think of a better way to share ideas, make personal and professional connections and generally have an extremely productive yet enjoyable time. That being said, the unconference format can be challenging and confusing, especially for those used to a more traditional conference model. Sharing some of my unconference experiences might make things a little easier.

Participation

Participation is by far the most important factor in determining whether or not an unconference will be successful. For the organizer, it is essential to get people together who truly want to be involved. For the attendee, an unconference is one of those situations where you really get back what you put in. The best sessions by far had the feel of an engaging graduate seminar class, with contributions coming from everyone, and where there was freedom for even the topic to evolve with the discussion. In other words, everyone came to participate.

I will also point out that while it's completely natural to spend the majority of your preparation time on your own presentation, my experience suggests that bringing thoughtful questions to other presentations is equally important. The best thing about an unconference is that professionals are able to come together and discuss real issues face to face. So don't lose sight of the fact that your input could be the difference between moving someone else's project forward—perhaps in ways they never expected. Related to this, make sure to pay attention to the other participants' blog/website postings and comments leading up to the conference—this, of course, being dependent on the unconference having a blog or website. Knowing what other people are thinking about before the event can jump-start discussion in a powerful way.

What to Propose?

Another common question for prospective unconference participants is what to propose. The most important thing I learned about unconference proposals, as both a presenter and an audience member, is that interactivity is essential. No one wants to sit around and be read to, especially when it's possible to give them a chance to react and share their own ideas.

Along with this, it cannot be stressed enough that big ideas should be welcome. Even if these ideas—as is often the case—are challenging to define, explain, or put into practical terms. Remember that because these discussions can be free-flowing, there is no need to arrive at the unconference with predetermined conclusions. Simply asking the interesting question is all that is required.

On the other hand, some great sessions were remarkably down-to-earth and practical. This was especially true when talking about technology, coding, implementation of new tools, etc. The point is, while big ideas are encouraged, practicality and pragmatism are also important components in many excellent proposals.

Enjoy Yourself

The unconference model allows for relatively informal discussions to take place. Also, because everyone is technically a presenter, many of the hierarchies found in some more traditional conferences are eased. I would advise everyone attending an unconference to take advantage of this. Make connections with people from different levels of seniority or experience. I've found that the more people enjoy themselves, the better the conversations flow, which, in turn, leads to better discussion and a more successful event. So have fun.

Let's Do It Already

—Jeremy Boggs

Many have loathed the rigidity, formality, and expense of traditional academic conferences. In contrast, unconferences thrive on flexibility, collegiality, and thrift. More to the point, they rely heavily on the attendees themselves—their attitudes, motivations, and work ethics—for success or failure. At unconferences, it generally doesn't matter who says something first; what matters more is who says something thoughtful, and what that thoughtful thing is. Discovery happens through group cooperation.

Insight and knowledge are not guarded for the next publication; they're shared openly, with hopes that others can contribute to ongoing conversations that make our work better.

This really gets to the heart of the issue: why do we attend conferences, and why do we contribute to them? Ideally, we give conference papers in hopes of sharing our research, getting recognition for such research, and getting critical feedback. We might also hope that conference paper's mere presence on the conference program grants it weight on CVs and tenure reviews, even if only half a dozen people actually came to the session to hear it read.

What if instead we start fostering systems that reward you if your unconference session spawns half a dozen projects from attendees? The focus in this case is not on what you produce yourself, but what you help others produce.

Academic conferences as they are now are increasingly expensive, poorly attended—not necessarily in terms of registrations, but in terms of people actually attending sessions—and rarely seem to generate the kind of innovative work needed to meet the challenges of education and scholarship today. If we want to start hacking the academy, let's start hacking this cornerstone of academic culture by incorporating unconference elements into the programs of traditional conferences. If you're going to an annual conference, try to organize an unconference yourself, either with support of the organization, or on your own off-site. We should start small; test some things out; make changes when necessary. But we should start, if for no other reason than to make the work we and our colleagues do better, and to make our experiences at conferences richer and more productive.

Voices

TWITTER AT CONFERENCES

Kathleen Fitzpatrick, Jason B. Jones,
Matthew G. Kirschenbaum, Amanda French

Buried within the sense that the 140-character form trivializes our work—a complaint about condensation that might not be so far removed from faulting poetry for its failure to present extended realist narratives—is an implied concern about who it is that sees us being trivial. This is a concern that has dogged public scholarly work for eons, from those scholars who have written crossover books, to those who have written editorials for major publications, to those who have developed blogs and other online presences. Yes, Twitter is the most elliptical of these, but it's a key form of outreach not just to our colleagues but to the broader intellectual public, and to those whom we need to support higher education. All of these public forms of writing have the potential to demonstrate what it is that we as scholars do, and why the broader culture should care about it—and until we get over our fears of talking with the broader culture, in the forms that we share with them, we'll never manage to convince them that what we do is important.

—KATHLEEN FITZPATRICK

Twitter is one way to explain to graduate students what you do at big conferences. In addition to the actual intellectual conversation, the critical mass of faculty on Twitter means that you can see what faculty do: how often people go to panels, when they visit the book exhibit, when they need downtime, whether they're still working on papers, and more. There's a comfort in seeing the different ways in which faculty and graduate students inhabit the conference: There's not just one way of participating in a conference, and so you should feel empowered to make the event as meaningful/productive for you as possible, without worrying too much about whether you're "doing it right."

—JASON B. JONES

Twitter is an invaluable ready-made network, particularly for newbies and junior scholars for whom the convention often looms like an orbital Death Star poised to suck every ion of individuality and intellectual self-worth into its all-consuming tractor beam. Twitter, by contrast, is the cantina in Mos Eisley spaceport. The "tweet-ups" are a great example of this: if you need a break, need a drink, or just need some time to turn off and chill out, you know when and where to go without the pressure and hang-ups of "Am I really invited?" "Will anyone talk to me?" Nothing in an institutionalized world is ever purely democratic or transparent of course, but I think it's fair to say that academic rank and status are markedly less important than if, say, you try sidling up to someone at the New Literary History cash bar. Most of all what I think Twitter does at a conference is create a common narrative; or better, it's a kind of communal narrative to which all can write simply by virtue of opening an account and invoking the hashtag. Retweets and replies define the plot and tempo. The narrative is not complete or comprehensive, but that's not the point. Narratives are enabling precisely because they are partial representations. Who knows this better than scholars?

—MATTHEW G. KIRSCHENBAUM

The lesson digital humanists learn, especially by using Twitter, is that scholarly conversations move quickly now, because they can; therefore, one had better be as quick as possible to join in that conversation. Monthly or quarterly journals and annual conferences used to be the way that scholars wrote among themselves, but now it's e-mail listservs—yes, still—and, better, the much more public blogosphere and Twittersphere.

—AMANDA FRENCH

The Entropic Library

Andrew Ashton

In the United States, over the past century, the practice of health care has transitioned from being a largely distributed and generalist profession to a much more corporatized and specialized one. It is a change that many greet with regret, despite the obvious advances in health care. One of our cultural touchstones is a romanticized image of the doctor or caregiver tending to patients in their homes; a leather satchel containing crucial instruments nearby. Still, we acknowledge a new reality—of health care as a consumer product: tranched and parsed into products designed for maximum efficiency. Home health care is considered a scarce and expensive resource. In other sectors, we see a similar trend. Local mechanics, hardware stores, and groceries are disappearing in favor of one-stop box stores. Geek Squad and Facebook are replacing specialists who used to fix computers in the home or provide websites for small businesses.

Academic libraries are different. They are, and have been for a long time, highly centralized institutions whose services and organizational structures are often designed to reflect a certain order that is perceived to exist within the broader institution.

Departments have liaisons, collection development often falls along disciplinary lines, and the library is treated as a destination—a physical and virtual domain—out of which the tools for scholarship will be doled. Academic libraries are faced with a challenge that is the inverse in other sectors: we are faced with a digital-scholarship environment that screams for decentralizing many library services. In order to do so, we must overcome a static cultural momentum.

In 2002, the American Library Association launched the massive Campaign for America's Libraries. The centerpiece of the campaign was a new marketing effort built around the slogan, "@ Your Library." According to the ALA's website, the campaign has several purposes.

> Promote awareness of the unique role of academic and research libraries and their contributions to society;

Increase visibility and support for academic and research libraries and librarians; help librarians better market their services on-site and online;

Position academic and research librarianship as a desirable career opportunity.[1]

While these are mostly admirable goals, they betray the extent to which the library profession, as represented by the ALA, is willing to respond to the challenges of the digital era by simply marketing traditional services more aggressively. This approach is flawed; not because patrons do not value traditional library services, but because the services no longer reflect the character of the institutions that they serve.

When the traditional disciplines engage more with digital technologies, the familiar practices become fragmented and less familiar—a phenomenon that Wendell Piez describes as akin to "a field where native plants and wildflowers are overtaking a tidy lawn." This unruliness disrupts the mappings that libraries have traditionally applied to the disciplines. Instead of designing liaison, cataloging, and collection-development services that support a predictable mode of scholarly work, libraries need to support scholarship that emerges from a state of relative entropy. The new mapping, in other words, is not to make traditional library services more digital, but rather to explode them out into a complementary state of entropy.

The entropic library is one in which the library is not only a physical destination and an institutional cornerstone, but also is a gravitational force in the digital scholarly life of the campus. It is a force that is exerted by library staff acting as consultants, software developers, funders, principal investigators, data curators, and mad scientists. It acts as a resource for the university's scholars by helping to shape and support new digital methodologies, which it channels into programmatic activities when there is a potential benefit to the wider university community. Its first concern is not to get digital things into the library as new collections, but to get the library to where the digital things are being used, and make them accessible and sustainable.

Embracing entropy is difficult for an institution whose identity has been defined by its advocacy of order, and it can be difficult for lovers of libraries to see entropy as anything but a threat to everything that we cherish in our libraries. Our romanticized image of the library tends to be of the library as a destination. In this image we might imagine the cloistered stacks, the hours spent ingesting the wisdom in the books, and the boundless potential in the unread volumes. It is a powerful image, and it is made more poignant by the sensory associations we often have with the library: the smell of the bindings, the muted sounds in the stacks, the concentration evident on the faces of readers. It is understandable that libraries, faced with the emergence of digital technologies in the 1990s, would design services that attempt to preserve the appeal of that library. Reference areas crammed with tables, lamps, and books transformed into computer labs, but the space retained its purpose as a destination for study and work. Card catalogs were replaced by Online Public Access Catalogs (OPACs), which were largely digital renditions of the same tools that libraries had always offered. Print-journal collections thinned as digital subscriptions became more cost-effective, although real challenges to the academic-publishing paradigm would not gain traction for at least another decade. The roles of librarians, however, largely remained the same—as gatekeepers and guides for information resources housed within and, to a limited extent, outside of the library's physical and digital bounds.

Creating digital surrogates for traditional services was a necessary, evolutionary step toward modernization. But there remains a chasm between the notion of the modern library as a purveyor of traditional resources delivered digitally, and the entropic library—steeped in and defined by the new digital scholarship. The entropic library needs to cultivate physical spaces in which to do scholarly work using digital media. Yet it is no longer a font from which information flows. It is a kaleidoscope of data, knowledge, and interaction, brought together by the scholarly primitives and crystallized for moments in the physical spaces that the university contains.

Note

1. "Welcome to the Academic and Research Library Campaign," *American Library Association*, http://www.ala.org/advocacy/advleg/publicawareness/campaign@yourlibrary/prtools/academicresearch/academicresearch.

The Wrong Business for Libraries

Christine Madsen

Our academic libraries have been in the wrong business for about 150 years. It was in the mid- to late nineteenth century that they began to be characterized as storehouses or warehouses of information. This information-centered model is a mistake. Before then, they were not stand-alone collections of books, but great complexes of mental and physical activity, and included museums, gymnasiums, and baths. The goal of the library was to support the great scholars of the day by providing them access to the most important sources of information, but also to everything else that was needed to turn that information into new knowledge—including a space for discourse and debate. Not that we should put baths or gymnasiums back in our libraries. We simply need to completely rethink both what it is that libraries do and why they do it.

The struggle of the academic library to stay relevant today is due to this switch from a scholar-centered model to an information-centered one. The imminent collapse of the latter model is causing tension not only across academic libraries and the field of library science, but across academia as a whole.

Prior to the Victorian era, most academic libraries were what Matthew Battles might characterize as Parnassan—small, well-focused institutions where what mattered was not the quantity of the collections, but the quality.[1] Then our system of universities exploded, and at the same time the cost of printing went down. Libraries began to put collecting at the top of their priorities. The result was that libraries changed from circumscribed institutions that fostered the entire life cycle of scholarship to what Andrew Abbott describes as a "universal identification, location, and access machine."[2] Where the Internet has made it possible to finally fulfill the idea of our university library as universal library (again, to use one of Battles's terms), our academic libraries have failed. In just a few short years, Google has come much closer to the creation of a universal library than our libraries have.

The problem is, of course, that we have spent nearly 150 years crafting this idea that our academic libraries are centers for information retrieval. Only one ALA-accredited graduate program has maintained the title "library science"; thirty have changed to "library and information science"; four put information first, but retain library—"information and library science"; and seventeen have dropped the library all together and are simply schools of "information science" or "information studies."[3] Similar trends can be seen in the United Kingdom, where most recently the program at University College London has changed from the department of "information and library science" to the department of "information studies." We don't even produce librarians anymore—we produce information scientists.

We librarians put all of our eggs into the "information basket" and it feels a bit late to turn back now. But the Internet has completely changed our relationship to information, and as a result, the model of library as information center is going to collapse.

It is time for a new theory of libraries—well past time, in fact. The user—the scholar—must be put back in the center of the academic research library again, but the users' needs must be considered within the broader context of the process of scholarship. In focusing on information, academic research libraries have, in part, been trying to address what users want, not what they need. As Ranganathan stated, "the majority of readers do not know their requirements."[4] It has long been the role of library and librarians to help scholars understand them.

The goal of any new theory of libraries must of course accommodate the increasing needs in research and scholarship for large quantities of information, but should not preface quantity of information over all else. As important as the information itself is, providing and supporting an environment that allows for the transformation of that information into new knowledge is essential.

What has been forgotten, for example, is that libraries were, and should be again, inherently social places. That these are spaces not just for getting access to resources, but to people—librarians, archivists, other scholars—with whom discourse can be entered about the resources therein. An academic research library should *first* be seen as a collection of services that support the creation of new knowledge. From this perspective, the library is not defined by its walls or by its collections, but by those very services. The goal of a library is not, then, to provide access to information, it is to provide a space—whether literal or virtual—for the support of all aspects of the scholarship process, with information provision being just one of these services. The information commons, gateway, or storehouse should not be the goal or the fate of the academic research library.

The library is a combination of tangible and intangible elements: a collection—of the tangible or digital—an organizational system, and scholarship, but also the invisible environment that contributes to and connects all three. There is no library, for example, without a culture of inquiry. Everything that is done in the library (entering, lingering, reflecting), and everything the library holds (collections of objects, living things, knowledge, information, contexts, lessons, memories), when bound together by a systematic, continuous, organized knowledge structure supports the act of new-knowledge creation known as scholarship. The result of the resources invested in the library, therefore, is not measured in the size of the collection, or even in the number or satisfaction of users, but in their experiences.

Notes

1. Matthew Battles, *Library: An Unquiet History* (W. W. Norton & Company, 2004).

2. Andrew Abbott, "Publication and the Future of Knowledge," 2008, http://home.uchicago.edu/%7Eaabbott/Papers/aaup.pdf.

3. American Library Association, "ALA: Alphabetical Accredited List," http://web.archive.org/web/20110605063115/http://www.ala.org/ala/educationcareers/education/accreditedprograms/directory/list/index.cfm.

4. S. R. Ranganathan, *Five Laws of Library Science*, 2nd ed. (Bombay: Asia Pub. House, 1963).

Reimagining Academic Archives

Christopher J. Prom

> 'Does the past exist concretely, in space? Is there somewhere or other a place, a world of solid objects, where the past is still happening?'
> 'No.'
> 'Then where does the past exist, if at all?'
> 'In records. It is written down.'
> 'In records. And—?'
> 'In the mind. In human memories.'
> 'In memory. Very well, then. We, the Party, control all records, and we control all memories."
>
> —GEORGE ORWELL, *Nineteen Eighty-Four*[1]

Archives are rarely created for the express purpose of being preserved, but develop organically as people live their—typically chaotic—lives. Archivists—many of whom serve in university archives and manuscript libraries—are dedicated to identifying, preserving, and providing access to a selective, authentic, and usable record of that messy human experience. People from all walks of life use archives to generate new ideas—or test existing ones—to confirm rights, to hold others accountable for their actions, to gain personal depth of understanding, to establish a connection with society or to the past, and to perform functions that help preserve democratic institutions, sustain civil society, or ensure social justice.

The archivist's charge was difficult enough to fulfill before the advent of networked computing technologies. Many people make overblown claims that a "digital dark age" is now upon us—that all of the electronic files we are creating will someday vanish. At first blush, we instinctively wonder how this could be possible: if there is one thing our lives do not lack, it is access to information. People demand, and are constantly developing better ways to control, index, and sort massive stores of information, but few believe that it will all someday vanish, or perhaps slowly rot away.

It is trite to say that e-mail, websites, blog entries, digital photographs, textual records, database files, and other electronic records are very susceptible to accidental loss, deletion, or decontextualization, even if we do not accept the premises of dystopian predictions that civilization will collapse after the oil runs out, or a catastrophe besets humanity. Nevertheless, records become more fragile and vulnerable as individuals, business, and even governments outsource data storage and management to the warm embrace of commercial vendors, ostensibly under the rubric of cost cutting and efficiency. Also, most people now create records using a wide range of tools, services, and hardware, leaving interrelated records strewn across hard drives, shared servers, social-networking sites, and cloud applications. These documents reside under the care, custody, and control of many different people and organizations—not simply the person or organization that created, and has a vested interest in, their content.

Leaving aside the factors mentioned above, every set of electronic records is itself a constructed and contested entity. The person who creates or assembles the documents molds them into an archive through their activities, interests, and sometimes, their malfeasance, subterfuge, or inertia. Those who control its means of access also have a chilling ability to shape how that record is presented to the public, as certain citizens of the People's Republic of China know all too well.

However one wishes to slice or dice technical issues related to the creation and management of records, we know for certain that it is impossible to construct accurate histories without accurate and faithful evidence of people's actions. Those who use archives can reconstruct or understand those actions only when records are maintained in an intellectually coherent fashion. The contextual relationships between the individual documents that comprise an individual or corporate entity's intellectual output must be preserved. Similarly, future users of archives need to know how the records they are using are related to records produced by other records creators. Given these facts, what types of organizations are best placed to serve as the long-term, trusted custodian of authentic, verifiable, and accurate electronic records?

It is tempting to think that the preservation of digital heritage can be left to those who provide the service of storing and disseminating the thoughts that we distill using keyboards, video cameras, or other digital devices. But to do this would leave the records at extreme risk of loss. At the eighth European Conference on Digital Archiving, Steve Bailey described this problem using an apt metaphor: Imagine if we had trusted the preservation of the records left by Samuel Pepys—the eighteenth-century London diarist—to those who produced his communication media: the stationer who sold him his notebooks, the tanner who sold him his vellum, and the cartographer who sold him the maps he carefully annotated.[2]

Of course, each of the businesses Pepys patronized has long since passed gently into the night. We believe that the same fate will not await Google, Facebook, or Twitter, but even if they manage to survive, what will happen to the content stored in minor services, on contracted webhosts? Tellingly, the terms of service for nearly every free platform or low-cost web host make absolutely no promises regarding digital preservation, or even the return of content to users in case of business failure. Catastrophic business failure is hardly beyond the realm of possibility, as a shareholder in Arthur Andersen will point out. Over a fifty-year period, Google is as vulnerable to social or economic change as the newspaper industry, or perhaps a revolt over its privacy policies may mortally wound it. Even now, its revenue stream is highly reliant on a single source of income: advertising sales.

The recent archiving deal announced between Twitter and the Library of Congress may or may not portend a partial solution to the problem of relying on commercial entities to preserve information needed for historical research. But let's not kid ourselves: the Library of Congress is extremely unlikely to strike deals with every commercial entity providing social-media services, much less every web host, in the country. Other factors will undermine the effectiveness of mass archives. Users, quite understandably and predictably, have already begun to assert a—self-declared—right to remove content from the Library of Congress. The Twitter terms of service put into effect on September 10, 2009, provides Twitter express permission to make tweets available to anyone they choose, and the disposition of public tweets made prior to this date, as well as all of the private tweets, should be an interesting issue for the California judicial system to resolve.

Even if the mass archiving of materials from millions of records creators did not face significant legal hurdles, the methods that libraries use to catalog and make information available are not well suited to preserving the full context necessary to make individual records understandable. To oversimplify at the risk of stereotyping: libraries deal well with items, such as books, or consistent runs of uniform media, such as serials; archives deal well with aggregations of mixed media, and with preserving the contextual information that make them understandable. While large repositories such as the Library of Congress can use cutting-edge tools to mine and repurpose large volumes of data, most tweets cannot be understood without extensive recourse to other online materials, such as blog posts or videos.

Using their professional principles of provenance, sanctity of original order, collective appraisal, and active custodianship, archivists possess the conceptual tools to preserve and make accessible the raw materials of future history: e-mail, digital photographs, and other electronic records. Unfortunately, most archives have made little systematic progress in identifying, preserving, and providing access to electronic records.

Why have most archives failed to effectively address electronic records issues? The reasons are many, but in the end the typical answers are that "digital preservation is hard," and "we don't have enough money to do it properly."

Nevertheless, working closely with university faculty, staff, and students, archivists must reorient archival programs toward electronic records, and to appropriate a set of low-cost tools and services to preserve digital information in a trustworthy fashion. The exact way in which local archives may choose to rethink, reconceptualize, reconstruct, or re-create itself will vary and must be shaped by local context, but almost any institution can cobble this together with existing open-source software. Ultimately, traditional archives must be reimagined in an act of constructive transformation.

Notes

1. George Orwell, *Nineteen Eighty-Four* (New York: Plume, 1949).
2. Steve Bailey, "In Whose Hands Does the Future of Digital Archiving Lie?," presented at the eighth European Conference on Digital Archiving, http://www.vsa-aas.org/de/aktuell/eca-2010/2010-4-29/.

Interdisciplinary Centers and Spaces

Stephen Ramsay and Adam Turner

Centers of Attention

—Stephen Ramsay

I've been around digital humanities centers for a long time—fifteen years at least. I've worked at them—in positions ranging from part-time staff member to Fellow—consulted for them, given speeches at various openings and anniversaries, and been present at a few center funerals. So, I'm always interested in how these things get started and how they end.

One of my favorite founding stories involves the Institute for Advanced Technology in the Humanities (IATH) at the University of Virginia, where a lot of my ideas about centers were formed. According to the story, IBM offered to donate a server to the University of Virginia—this was back when such things were much rarer, and a lot more expensive. The university naturally approached the computer science department, asking if they'd like the equipment. The department, amazingly, said "no." They had heard, however, that there were some people over in the English and history departments who were doing things with computers. Maybe ask them.

I've always imagined the server washing up on the shores of the College of Arts and Sciences and starting a strange cargo cult among a group of people who normally didn't talk to each other much. There's a guy in history who's into computers, and there's someone in English. Neither of them really knows what they're doing, and the computer science people are too busy with serious computational matters to help out the poets. The librarians, fortunately, know more than the computer scientists about how to actually run a rack server, and so they get involved. Questions arise: Where do we put this thing? Who pays for its upkeep? Doesn't it need, like, maintenance or witchcraft, or something? Are we really qualified to design websites, given that none of us have the faintest idea how to draw?

That this turned into one of the most vibrant centers of intellectual activity in North America—a hugely influential research group that would be widely imitated by such contemporary powerhouses as the Maryland Institute for Technology in the Humanities and the University of Nebraska–Lincoln's Center for Digital Research in the Humanities—should surprise no one.

We like to marvel at the technological wonders that proceed from things like servers, but in this case—I would say, in all cases—the miracle of "computers in the humanities" is the way it forced even a highly balkanized academy into new kinds of social formations. Anyone involved with any of these big centers will tell you that they are rare sites of genuine collaboration and intellectual synergy—that they explode disciplinary boundaries and even the cherished hierarchies of academic rank. They do this, because . . . well, really because no one really knows what they're doing. Because *both* the English professor and the history professor need to learn MySQL; because the undergraduate student from art history happens to be the only one who knows PHP; because actually, you do need to learn how to draw—or at least know something about design—and the designers are pleased to reveal their art to you. Because you know Java.

These may not sound like disruptive modalities, but in an area of scholarship where coauthorship is viewed with suspicion and collaboration is rare, the idea that you couldn't master everything necessary to create a digital archive or write a piece of software was a complete revelation. It forced scholars to imagine their activities in terms of highly interdependent groups. To succeed, you had to become like the Clerk in *The Canterbury Tales*; "gladly would he learn and gladly would he teach." Working as a full-time programmer at IATH in the late 1990s—while finishing a PhD in English—not only changed the way I think about computers in the humanities, but changed the way I think about the humanities, and about higher education itself.

Universities are designed around subject areas. But what if they were designed, like centers, around methodologies or even questions? Right now, we have English departments, and political science departments, and biology departments. These various units—made up of people who only occasionally talk to each other—band off to form things like the Graduate Certificate Program in Eighteenth-Century French Drama, or the Center for Peace Studies, or the Bioinformatics Initiative. What would it be like if that was all there was—structures meant to bring people and students together for as long as a methodology remains useful or a question remains interesting? Such entities would be born like centers—born with all the excitement and possibility of not knowing what you're doing—of having to learn from each other what the methodologies and questions are really about. They might also die like centers. I mentioned that I've been at a few center funerals, and I can tell you that they don't die the way you think—lack of funding, for example, is probably the least common reason. Mostly, they die because people move on to other questions and concerns—and what's wrong with that? You could imagine a university in which scholars move through a number of different centers over the course of a career, and students pass through a number of them on the way to a degree—we'd have to change the names of the degrees to something vague, like "Bachelor of Arts" or "Doctor of Philosophy."

Years ago, while working at IATH, my dissertation director—Jerome McGann, one of the cargo cult founders—stopped me in the hallway and said, "Steve, be sure to treasure this experience. I've worked in this field a long time, and I can tell you: you may never see this again." I think Jerry was right and wrong about that. He was wrong; I've managed to see it several times since leaving IATH, most especially at the center I'm now involved with—the Center for Digital Research in the Humanities. But he was also right. It's easy to treasure the wrong thing about digital centers: to see the excitement brewing in a community of teachers, students, and researchers as a new opportunity for what we might do, rather than a way to affirm an amazing thing that has already happened.

Hacker Spaces as Scholarly Spaces

—Adam Turner

A hallmark of the hacker/maker culture is community collaboration. That community is often physically manifest in a particular space—a rented warehouse, a shed, somebody's garage. Hacker spaces often grow out of a common need for a place to work, exchange ideas, share knowledge, and pool resources. In these cases, the community essentially exists without the space, but it is the space that breathes life into the community. Interdisciplinary practice works in much the same way. Many in academia are already interested in—and often work across—multiple disciplines, but lack a common space to facilitate both independent disciplinary work and collaborative interdisciplinary work. A hacker space.

Such a scholarly space—of which HUMLab, the digital humanities and new-media lab at Umea University in Sweden, serves as an excellent established example—exists not to institute interaction, but to provide a creative environment for scholars, researchers, artists, students, teachers, anyone with interest (hence paradisciplinary), to work, exchange ideas, share knowledge, and pool resources. A flexible scholar/hacker space encourages exchange of ideas, collaboration, and discovery beyond the discipline through an organic process of interaction, sharing, and learning from each other. Possibly the most valuable aspect of such a space would be the creation of a hacker/scholar/maker community in which members are free to pursue their own research and academic projects, and also to collaborate and interact with the community as a whole.

Like a discipline, such a community would provide a living repository of common knowledge and quality practice, but instead of establishing a single shared heuristic, it would serve as a dynamic collection of varied modes of thinking and questioning. This model is certainly not for everyone, and would likely not replace the current disciplinary model, but should it? One of the strengths of the hacker/maker model is that it is not an attempt to eliminate previous models so much as it represents a drive to modify and improve upon elements of those models.

In conjunction with a more flexible disciplinary framework, paradisciplinary scholar spaces could provide an organic—and fun—means of thinking and doing across the academic disciplinary divide. Hacking is about doing: creating, thinking, questioning, observing, learning, and teaching. The core of academic work is, at its heart, hacking. The scholar-hacker takes this and runs with it; breaking open previous modes of thought to see how they tick, rearranging them, adding to them, and then taping, soldering, and gluing them back together again.

Take an Elective

Sharon Leon

Tasked with establishing a university for Catholics in Ireland in the 1850s, Cardinal John Henry Newman distilled his understanding of the university as a place for teaching, learning, and conversation where inquiry is pushed forward. Though Newman was focused on the undergraduate education of men, by men, his insights hold import for all of us, including those of us with advanced degrees. Newman discussed the importance of exposing students to many perspectives in his essay, "The Idea of a University."

> . . . the drift and meaning of a branch of knowledge varies with the company in which it is introduced to the student. If his reading is confined simply to one subject, however such division of labour may favour the advancement of a particular pursuit . . . certainly it has a tendency to contract his mind. If it is incorporated with others, it depends on those others as to the kind of influence which it exerts upon him. . . .
>
> It is a great point then to enlarge the range of studies which a University professes, even for the sake of the students; and, though they cannot pursue every subject which is open to them, they will be the gainers by living among those and under those who represent the whole circle. This I conceive to be the advantage of a seat of universal learning, considered as a place of education. An assemblage of learned men, zealous for their own sciences, and rivals of each other, are brought, by familiar intercourse and for the sake of intellectual peace, to adjust together the claims and relations of their respective subjects of investigation. They learn to respect, to consult, to aid each other. Thus is created a pure and clear atmosphere of thought, which the student also breathes, though in his own case he only pursues a few sciences out of the multitude.[1]

Thus, this effort to produce well-rounded human beings rather than intensely specialized practitioners appeared to have significant benefits for both the students and the faculty.

If we are to consider how we might change the practices of the academy to help us begin to move past a place of systemic dysfunction, we have to propose solutions that seem realistic to both junior and senior faculty in more traditional positions. How? *Take an elective.* Embrace eclecticism, and give yourself permission to dedicate some percentage of your week to learning or investigating something completely new, in the service of having more intellectual fun.

Remember what it felt like to take an elective that truly excited you? Remember the joy of doing something just because it was fun and challenging, in and of itself? Perhaps this is a scholarly version of Google's 20 percent rule, where employees get one day a week to work on their own projects. But since as academics we are mostly self-directed, this time be dedicated to moving beyond the core forms of individual work that are the benchmarks of disciplinary promotion and tenure. Consider a new methodological approach. Produce work that takes a nontraditional form. Work with colleagues from other disciplines. Then, step forward and proclaim the results as being central to the future health and welfare of the academy. This elective work has the potential to enlarge the way that we think about and evaluate scholarship. Thus, it can remind the academy as a whole that the value of our work is not that it results in a monograph or a bevy of articles in major scholarly journals, but that it opens up new lines of inquiry and pushes our collective understanding of the world forward.

Note

1. John Henry Newman, "The Idea of a University," *Newman Reader*, September 2001, http://www.newmanreader.org/works/idea/index.html, 100–101.

Voices

INTERDISCIPLINARITY

Ethan Watrall, Kathleen Fitzpatrick, David Parry

Many institutions pride themselves on encouraging interdisciplinary scholarship. However, the reality is that it is much easier to have a traditional, one-field identity—e.g., English, geology, physics, etc.—than it is to create and maintain an interdisciplinary identity. The very structure of most universities is based on a model of one scholar, one discipline—the unit of discipline being the department. Departments are usually walled gardens, little islands of thought and practice that are surrounded by moats filled with sharks, and patrolled by giant killer robots with instructions to kill on sight. (What? Your department doesn't have giant killer robots?)

—ETHAN WATRALL

Debates about field definition are often less about determining what good work in a field might be than they are about turf wars—turf wars driven less by intellectual questions than by institutional and economic imperatives. I wonder about the cost of that disciplinarity; about the degree to which we are now being disciplined by our need to define the field. What conversations won't take place, now that our structure has become officially institutionalized? I hope that we can find a way—and perhaps a way that might model a new mode of interdisciplinary affiliation for the university at large—to imagine our borders less as walled structures than as the containing elements of Venn diagrams, somehow semipermeable, allowing for overlap and intermingling, rather than producing territorial invasion and defense.

—KATHLEEN FITZPATRICK

If what the digital does is just take the old disciplines and make them digital, leaving disciplinarity and the silo structure of the university intact, it will have failed. I want to see the digital transform not just the content or practice of the disciplines, but the very idea of disciplinarity.

—DAVID PARRY

Cautions

An Open Letter to the Forces of Change

Jennifer Howard

To: The forces of change
From: J. Howard

So you want to hack the academy? I can't tell you how to do it. I can ask you a few well-intentioned questions, though, because journalists ask questions. These are a few that have occurred to me as I do what I do: write about academic publishing; go to conferences; talk to scholars, editors, publishers, and librarians; and generally get my feet wet in the fast-flowing, ever-shifting river of scholarly communication. These are questions lobbed at you from the sidelines, not from the trenches. I'm an observer, not a specialist, which may make these useful or may not. Either way, I'm curious to see the results of your experiment.

1) *What do you mean by that?* Or: beware the language of the oppressor. I keep a running list in my head of phrases I hear so often they no longer mean anything. For instance, can you break down "adding value" for me? If you're not an employee of NORAD or a grain farmer, do you really need to talk about "silos"? And on and on. Every field has its vocabulary and a rhetoric by which it recognizes itself; every discipline and every trade, including mine, has a shorthand: that's useful—and limiting. It's good to keep an eye on when useful has given way to limiting, especially if you're trying to remake the world. A fresh message requires a fresh vocabulary—or a freshening up of the old one. If you come up with a handy alternative to the phrase "the dissemination of research" please let me know, because I sure could use one.

2) *How do you keep crowdsourcing from becoming another in crowd?* This is tricky. A revolution does not succeed without like-minded souls, compadres, and comrades-in-arms working together. How do you create alternative forms of authority without creating an alternative regime? Are you opening the gates or shutting them? Storming the barricades or erecting new ones? Will the next generation—or those who feel excluded from the conversation—be tempted to bring out the tumbrels for you?

3) *Have you looked for friends in the enemy camp lately?* Or: maybe you will find allies where you don't expect any. As a journalist, I'm no stranger to generalizations. Still, it's disconcerting to go to different conferences and hear Entire Category X—administrators/university presses/librarians/journal editors/fill in the blank—written off as part of the problem when at least a few daring souls might not mind being part of a solution. It may not be *your* solution. You might have to venture a closer look to find out. I can't say what you will discover. It may not be at all what you expect. It might be exactly what you expect. Let me know.

The Trouble with Digital Culture

Tim Carmody

One of the problems with studying any medium is that it's too easy to mistake the part for the whole. Literature professors can confidently chart the development of the novel over centuries by referencing only a tiny well-regarded sliver of all novels published—some immensely popular, and others forgotten. When you turn to the broader field of print culture, books jostle against newspapers, advertisements, letters, memos, government and business forms, postcards, sheet music, reproduced images, money, business cards and nameplates, and thousands of other forms that have little if anything to do with the codex book. We tend toward influential, fractional exemplars, partly out of necessity (raised to the level of institutions) and partly out of habit (raised to the level of traditions). Yet trouble inevitably arises when we forget that the underexamined whole exists, or pretend that it doesn't matter. It always does. If nothing else, the parts that we cut out for special scrutiny draw their significance in no small part by how they relate to the other, subterranean possibilities.

The culture of digital technology, like that of print, is impressively broad, thoroughly differentiated, and ubiquitously integrated into most of our working and nonworking lives. This makes it difficult for media scholars and historians to study, just as it makes it difficult—but inevitable—for scholars to recognize how this technology has changed, is changing, and should continue to change the academy. Self-professed digital humanists—and I consider myself one—generally look at digital culture, then identify themselves and model their practices on only a sliver of the whole.

Digital culture far exceeds the World Wide Web, social networks, e-books, image archives, games, e-mail, and programming codes. It exceeds anything we see on our laptops, phones, or television screens. It even exceeds the programmers, hackers, pirates, clerics, artists, electricians, and engineers who put that code into practice, and the protocols, consoles, and infrastructure that govern and enable their use.

This is important, because digital humanists' efforts to "hack the academy" most often turn out *not* to be about replacing an established analog set of practices and institutions with new digital tools and ideas; instead, it's a battle within digital culture itself: the self-styled "punk" culture of hackers, pirates, coders, and bloggers against the office suite, the management database, the IT purchaser. Twitter vs. the university's e-mail system. These are also reductions, but potentially instructive ones.

For my own part, I tend to see digital humanism less as a matter of individual or group identity, or the application of digital tools to materials and scholarship in the humanities, but instead as something that is happening, continuing to emerge, develop, and differentiate itself, both inside and outside of the academy, as part of the spread of information and the continual redefinition of our assumptions about how we encounter media, as well as technological and other objects in the world. In this, every aspect of digital technology—whether old or new, establishment or counterestablishment—plays a part.

Contributors

Andrew Ashton is the Director of Digital Technologies at Brown University Library.

Jon Beasley-Murray is an Associate Professor in Hispanic Studies at the University of British Columbia.

Chad Black is an Associate Professor of Early Latin American History at the University of Tennessee–Knoxville.

Jeremy Boggs is the Design Architect for Digital Research and Scholarship at the University of Virginia Library.

Gideon Burton is an Assistant Professor of English at Brigham Young University.

James Calder is Digital Humanities Specialist at the Ohio Humanities Council.

Gardner Campbell is an Associate Professor of English and the Director of Professional Development and Innovative Initiatives at Virginia Tech.

Tim Carmody is a Senior Writer at *The Verge*.

Larry Cebula is an Associate Professor of History at Eastern Washington University.

Daniel J. Cohen is the Director of the Roy Rosenzweig Center for History and New Media and an Associate Professor of History at George Mason University.

Brian Croxall is the Digital Humanities Strategist in the Robert W. Woodruff Library and Lecturer of English at Emory University.

Cathy Davidson is the Ruth F. DeVarney Professor of English and the John Hope Franklin Humanities Institute Professor of Interdisciplinary Studies at Duke University.

David Doria is a doctoral candidate in Electrical Engineering at Rensselaer Polytechnic Institute.

Kathleen Fitzpatrick is the Director of Scholarly Communication at the Modern Language Association.

Amanda French is a Research Assistant Professor and THATCamp Coordinator at the Roy Rosenzweig Center for History and New Media at George Mason University.

Anne Ellen Geller is an Associate Professor of English and Director of Writing Across the Curriculum at the Institute for Writing Studies at St. John's University.

Matt Gold is the Director of the CUNY Academic Commons and Associate Professor at the New York City College of Technology and CUNY Graduate Center.

Jim Groom is the Director of the Division of Teaching and Learning Technologies and Adjunct Professor at the University of Mary Washington.

Jo Guldi is a Junior Fellow at the Harvard Society of Fellows.

Jennifer Howard is a Senior Reporter at the *Chronicle of Higher Education.*

Jason Baird Jackson is an Associate Professor of Folklore in the Department of Folklore and Ethnomusicology at Indiana University Bloomington.

Jeff Jarvis is an Associate Professor and Director of the Tow-Knight Center for Entrepreneurial Journalism at the City University of New York's Graduate School of Journalism.

Jason B. Jones is a Professor of English at Central Connecticut State University.

Rey Junco is a Faculty Associate at the Berkman Center for Internet and Society at Harvard University.

Mills Kelly is an Associate Professor of History at George Mason University.

Matthew G. Kirschenbaum is an Associate Professor of English at the University of Maryland, College Park.

Sharon Leon is the Director of Public Projects at the Roy Rosenzweig Center for History and New Media and Research Associate Professor at George Mason University.

Christine Madsen is the Manager of Infrastructure and Innovation in the Digital Library Systems and Services division of the Bodleian Libraries at the University of Oxford.

Jeff McClurken is Chair and Associate Professor of History and American Studies at the University of Mary Washington.

Bethany Nowviskie is the Director of Digital Research and Scholarship, including the Scholars' Lab, at the University of Virginia Library.

Michael O'Malley is an Associate Professor of History at George Mason University.

David Parry is an Assistant Professor of Emerging Media and Communications at the University of Texas at Dallas.

Christopher J. Prom is the Assistant University Archivist and Associate Professor of Library Administration at the University of Illinois at Urbana–Champaign.

Stephen Ramsay is an Associate Professor of English at the University of Nebraska–Lincoln.

Anastasia Salter is an Assistant Professor in the Division of Science, Information Arts and Technologies at the University of Baltimore.

Mark Sample is an Associate Professor in the Department of English at George Mason University.

Tom Scheinfeldt is Director-at-Large at the Roy Rosenzweig Center for History and New Media and a Research Assistant Professor at George Mason University.

Kelly Schrum is Director of Educational Projects at the Roy Rosenzweig Center for History and New Media and an Associate Professor in the Higher Education Program at George Mason University.

Tad Suiter is a doctoral candidate in History at George Mason University.

Adam Turner is a doctoral candidate in History at the University of Oregon.

John Unsworth is the Vice-Provost for Library and Technology Services and Chief Information Officer at Brandeis University.

Adrianne Wadewitz is a Postdoctoral Fellow at the Center for Digital Learning and Research at Occidental College.

Ethan Watrall is an Assistant Professor of Anthropology and Associate Director of MATRIX at Michigan State University.

Michael Wesch is an Associate Professor of Cultural Anthropology at Kansas State University.